PRAISE FO

Abandon

A Junior Library Guil

"The authors do an excellent job of conveying the chaos and loss of this grisly historical incident without pushing young readers too deeply into the horror. Archival photos add immediacy to this sensational true-life story."
—*The Wall Street Journal*

"An amazing account of a World War II event that is almost entirely unknown.... This story chronicles the courage, compassion, and perseverance of the few survivors of the incident, showcasing war at its worst and humanity at its best.... School librarians will want to add this to their collection." —*Booklist*

"Through viscerally told accountings, including stories of passengers spending several days awaiting rescue aboard lifeboats, the authors deliver a fascinating tale of human perseverance and morality that explores the 'most unusual actions in all of World War II,' as stated by the creators in an introduction." —*Publishers Weekly*

"In contrast to the usual run of shipwreck tales built around the simple theme of 'heroic survival against the odds,' this account depicts the 1942 torpedoing of the British liner *Laconia* as a realistically messy mix of confusion, desperation, altruism, cruelty, and extreme hardship." —*Booklist*

"The unbiased narrative follows the personal stories of the real men, women, and children moved to German ships or abandoned in lifeboats on the open ocean. Ideal for WWII history fans and readers who have graduated from Lauren Tarshis's 'I Survived' series." —*School Library Journal*

"This epic story races along, unspooling like a movie before our eyes—artfully, dramatically, revealing a little known part of WWII history. An intriguing book." —Doug Stanton, #1 *New York Times* bestselling author of *In Harm's Way*

ABANDON SHIP!

THE TRUE WORLD WAR II STORY ABOUT THE SINKING OF THE *LACONIA*

BY MICHAEL J. TOUGIAS

TRUE SURVIVAL SERIES

Abandon Ship!
(cowritten with Alison O'Leary)

Fatal Forecast

TRUE RESCUE SERIES

The Finest Hours

A Storm Too Soon

Into the Blizzard

Attacked at Sea
(cowritten with Alison O'Leary)

In Harm's Way
(Young Readers Adaptation of Doug Stanton's
In Harm's Way)

TRUE SURVIVAL SERIES

ABANDON SHIP!

THE TRUE WORLD WAR II STORY ABOUT THE SINKING OF THE *LACONIA*

MICHAEL J. TOUGIAS
& ALISON O'LEARY

Christy Ottaviano Books
LITTLE, BROWN AND COMPANY
New York Boston

Interior art credits: Ship deck © sandsun/Shutterstock.com; ship water trail © LIUSHENGFILM/Shutterstock.com; sunken ship steering wheel © A Daily Odyssey/Shutterstock.com; knot vector © KsushaArt/Shutterstock.com.

Cover art copyright © 2023 by Shane Rebenschied. Cover design by Jenny Kimura.
Cover copyright © 2023 by Hachette Book Group, Inc.
Interior design by Carla Weise

Christy Ottaviano Books
Hachette Book Group
1290 Avenue of the Americas, New York, NY 10104
Visit us at LBYR.com

Originally published in hardcover and ebook by
Little, Brown and Company in February 2023
First Trade Paperback Edition: September 2024

Christy Ottaviano Books is an imprint of Little, Brown and Company. The Christy Ottaviano Books name and logo are trademarks of Hachette Book Group, Inc.

The Library of Congress has cataloged the hardcover edition as follows:
Names: Tougias, Michael J., 1955– author. | O'Leary, Alison, author.
Title: Abandon ship! : the true World War II story about the sinking of the Laconia / by New York Times–bestselling author Michael J. Tougias, and Alison O'Leary.
Description: First edition. | New York : Christy Ottaviano Books, Little, Brown and Company, 2023. | Series: True survival series | Includes bibliographical references. | Audience: Ages 9–14 |
Summary: "A remarkable true WWII account of the maritime attack on the RMS *Laconia* off the West African coast." —Provided by publisher.
Identifiers: LCCN 2022039644 | ISBN 9780316401371 (hardcover) | ISBN 9780316401579 (ebook)
Subjects: LCSH: Laconia (Steamship : 1921–1942)—Juvenile literature. | Steamboat disasters—Atlantic Ocean—History—20th century—Juvenile literature. | World War, 1939–1945—Search and rescue operations—Juvenile literature. | World War, 1939–1945—Naval operations, German—Juvenile literature. | Submarines (Ships)—Germany—History—20th century—Juvenile literature. | World War, 1939–1945—Naval operations—Submarine—Juvenile literature.
Classification: LCC D772.L23 T68 2023 |
DDC 940.54/293—dc23/eng/20220824
LC record available at https://lccn.loc.gov/2022039644

ISBNs: 978-0-316-40147-0 (trade paperback), 978-0-316-40157-9 (ebook)

Printed in Indiana, USA

LSC-C

Printing 2, 2024

TO PAUL LORRAINE, ADAM GAMBLE,
AND MARK & BOB TOUGIAS
—M. T.

TO KATHRYN O'LEARY, A TRUE
SURVIVOR AND TRUSTED ADVISER
—A. O.

CONTENTS

MAIN CHARACTERS AND VESSELS

SHIPS AND SUBMARINES

Laconia—six-hundred-foot British ship that carried 2,730 people, including the crew, military men, women and children, Italian POWs, and Polish guards

Gloire—588-foot French cruiser sent to rescue survivors of the sinking *Laconia*

U-boat 156—German U-boat that sank the *Laconia*

U-boat 506, U-boat 507, and *Cappellini*—three submarines that assisted in the rescue

LACONIA PASSENGERS AND CREW

Rudolph Sharp—captain of the *Laconia*

Claude Parr—young British crew member of the *Laconia*

Molly Davidson—nineteen-year-old civilian aboard *Laconia*

Josephine Frame—fourteen-year-old civilian aboard *Laconia*

Doris Hawkins—thirty-one-year-old civilian nurse aboard *Laconia*

Tony Large—nineteen-year-old sailor in the Royal Navy aboard *Laconia*

Jim McLoughlin—twenty-year-old sailor in the Royal Navy who operated a deck gun on the *Laconia*

Dr. Geoffrey Purslow—twenty-six-year-old surgeon on the *Laconia*

Harry Vines—gunner on the *Laconia*, in his twenties

Lady Grizel Wolfe-Murray—passenger aboard the *Laconia*

Ted Dobson—able seaman in Royal Navy, approximately twenty-five years old

Ted Riley—able seaman in the Royal Navy, in his early twenties

George, Ena, and June Stoneman—Royal Air Force sergeant and his family returning home from overseas assignment

A. J. Baldwin—lieutenant colonel in British army who was in charge of Italian prisoners

Thomas Buckingham—*Laconia*'s senior third officer, who was taken prisoner on U-507

GERMAN U-BOAT ADMIRAL AND COMMANDERS

Werner Hartenstein—commander of U-156

Karl Dönitz—admiral in charge of all U-boats

Harro Schacht—commander of U-507

Erich Würdemann—commander of U-506

ITALIAN SUBMARINE COMMANDER

Marco Revedin—commander of *Cappellini*

US ARMY AIR FORCE PERSONNEL

Captain Robert C. Richardson III—twenty-four-year-old commander of the First Composite Squadron on Ascension Island

Lieutenant James D. Harden—twenty-four-year-old pilot of the B-24 Liberator that bombed submarine U-156 while it was aiding *Laconia* survivors

INTRODUCTION

World War II began when Nazi Germany invaded Poland in 1939 and Great Britain and France tried to halt the Nazi takeover of Europe. The United States did not join the war until December 7, 1941, when Imperial Japan attacked the US naval base at Pearl Harbor, Hawaii. After the bombing of Pearl Harbor, Germany, Italy, and Japan (the Axis powers) all declared war on the United States, and the United States responded by declaring war on them.

Germany's submarines, called U-boats (undersea boats or, in German, *Unterseeboot*), were particularly effective tools of war. In the early months of the war, U-boats entered the channels surrounding Britain and torpedoed ships, some carrying crucial supplies from Canada. Residents of Great Britain nearly starved in the aftermath. From the fall of 1939 to the summer of 1940, as Germany invaded countries in Northern Europe, over five hundred ships were sunk around Britain and in the North Sea. Those numbers would grow—and fears grew with them.

This was a time for the U-boat captains to improve their torpedo skills. Having cracked the codes for secret British messages to ships moving goods and materials across the North Atlantic, the submarine force terrorized sailors. U-boats found nighttime best for evading detection. They surfaced unexpectedly, unleashing deadly attacks in the midst of a convoy of ships.

"The only thing that ever really frightened me during the war was the U-boat peril," British Prime Minister Winston Churchill wrote in his memoir.

When France surrendered to Germany in 1940, the Germans gained a strategic foothold; they built U-boat "pens," or home bases, along the French coast that allowed more efficient travel across the ocean to the United States. Along with shaving hundreds of miles off the transatlantic route, these pens were constructed to withstand punishing bomb attacks. On the French coast the Germans kept many long-range submarines. They were capable of spending approximately eight weeks at sea on missions exceeding ten thousand nautical miles without refueling.

Werner Hartenstein, a lieutenant commander in the German navy (Kriegsmarine), was in charge of one of these long-range U-boats, U-156. Hartenstein was patrolling waters five hundred miles off West Africa near the Equator in 1942 when he spotted the *Laconia*, a British ship. He maneuvered his sub into position to fire torpedoes and sink the ship.

The events that transpired next were among the most unusual actions in all of World War II and began a survival story like no other.

Part I

LACONIA BEFORE THE TORPEDOES

THE VOYAGE

LACONIA AND CAPTAIN SHARP

August 1942

Port Tawfiq, Egypt, simmered in the summer sun of mid-August 1942. At the harbor east of Cairo was the six-hundred-foot British ship *Laconia*. It had discharged thousands of British troops to fight German soldiers in North Africa. Now, under the watchful eye of Captain Rudolph Sharp, the *Laconia* was being loaded with provisions and passengers. Plans called for a long voyage of nearly fourteen thousand nautical miles with many ports of call.

The ship was once a luxury ocean liner that plied the waters between Liverpool, England, and New York. In September 1939 the *Laconia* was requisitioned by the British government for war use as a convoy escort, then a troopship. Defensive guns were mounted on the ship's deck, and the entire vessel was painted a dull gray. Attractive staterooms were converted to bunk rooms to accommodate as many people as possible, leaving the intercontinental liner little of its former glory. In recognition of the dangers the ship might encounter at sea, some cargo areas had been filled with hollow steel drums. It was hoped the drums would help keep the ship afloat if the hull was pierced by a torpedo.

Usually a ship like the *Laconia* would travel in a convoy with other ships for protection during wartime. These ships would be accompanied by a contingent of navy ships with crews highly experienced in detecting and reacting to enemy threats. But now most navy ships were aiding the military invasion elsewhere in Africa, and there was no convoy for *Laconia* to join. For this voyage, the ship would travel alone. This would prove to be a fatal mistake.

When the *Laconia* passengers settled in and the gangplank was removed, the ship began its six-week voyage to Britain. *Laconia* would steam south down the east coast of Africa, round the tip of the continent, and pass the Cape of Good Hope before traveling north far off Africa's west coast.

How many passengers knew that the *Laconia* shared a name with a ship that was sunk by German torpedoes in 1917 is anyone's guess. Yet at this point in the war everyone was familiar with the hazards posed by the dreadfully effective German U-boats. Each passenger was issued a life belt and urged to keep it within reach.

Lifeboat drills were a regular part of everyday life at sea. When a whistle sounded, passengers were required to assemble near their assigned lifeboats. The boats were mounted on the very top deck of the ship near the bridge, where the captain worked. Passengers learned a few basics about how to climb aboard lifeboats as they were lowered to the water. These drills were orderly and calm, unlike a real emergency.

One passenger who knew the dangers of sea travel quite well was Royal Navy Able Seaman Tony Large. His last ship, the cruiser *Cornwall*, had been bombed by Japanese planes and sunk in the Indian Ocean. He survived by clinging to debris in the water for twenty-four hours before another ship rescued him. Tony was hoping for better luck on this voyage.

Tony Large was one of 268 British sailors, soldiers, and airmen aboard the *Laconia,* which carried a crew of 460. Also on board were 80 civilian women and children and 1,793 Italian prisoners of war, with 102 Polish guards, for a total of 2,732 people when the ship left Cape Town.

The 19,695-ton *Laconia* had seven decks. Lower-ranking airmen and sailors like Tony were assigned bunks and a dining room in the more crowded lower, or third-class, portion of the ship. Officers of the army and Royal Air Force had their own areas for dining and recreation, near the middle of the ship. The highest-level officers and civilians, including all the women and children, were in the first-class quarters near the upper decks, where there was more space. One of the first-class passengers was a missionary nurse, Doris Hawkins, who was traveling with the fourteen-month-old daughter of Colonel Tim Readman and his wife. Involved in the war in the Middle East, the couple was sending their toddler to her grandparents in Britain. A handful of men evacuating due to war wounds were under the care of the ship's doctor. Except during lifeboat drills, few passengers mingled outside their assigned sections of the ship.

Locked in the deepest recesses of the *Laconia* were the Italian prisoners, essentially caged in large numbers in several cargo compartments. These men had been captured fighting British forces in North Africa and were destined for POW camps in the British countryside. The cramped quarters didn't allow hammocks to stretch without bumping into a neighbor. Their Polish guards had guns but no access to ammunition, making their authority questionable. Other passengers watched the Italians with curiosity when the guards escorted them on deck for brief periods of exercise and public showers with buckets of cold seawater.

About three weeks into the trip, one British army officer, Lieutenant Colonel A. J. Baldwin, was asked to inspect the Italian prisoners. "Conditions were disgusting," Baldwin observed. He went on to describe filthy bedding and dirty food containers. "Prisoners appeared overcrowded and the air, to my mind, insufficient. The atmosphere seemed foul and one had to get near the air vents to breathe properly." He noted that portholes were screwed shut in these lower holds of the ship. This worsened the humid, unhealthy conditions among the prisoners.

Baldwin found that guards frequently punished the entire group when one or two broke rules, such as smoking inside the ship. Baldwin immediately ended the group punishments, allowed prisoners to use indoor shower rooms, and started improving conditions.

When *Laconia* stopped in Cape Town, at the tip of Africa, passengers enjoyed the port's many shops and abundant goods. They made purchases for family and friends in Britain who had suffered shortages. During the war many items in Britain were scarce or rationed because the materials were needed for the army and navy. Items such as butter, meat, leather shoes, wool, and rubber tires were almost impossible to find or purchase in Britain.

Laconia's Captain Sharp knew that the southern route around Africa was safer than sailing through the Mediterranean Sea, where there were more German vessels. Captain Sharp thought it unlikely that U-boats would discover a ship traveling alone in the vast Atlantic Ocean. He would take precautions such as not allowing lights on at night and not transmitting radio signals that could be traced. The ship's guns, however, boomed from time to time and could easily be heard if the enemy was nearby. Captain Sharp thought it was a risk worth taking so that the gunners could practice using the weapons, firing shells at imaginary enemies to keep the crews ready. The captain could control some aspects of *Laconia*'s visibility, but it was impossible to prevent the telltale black smoke belching from the ship's single stack.

The *Laconia* left Cape Town on September 1 and began the journey north toward Great Britain. Captain Sharp's precautions, particularly *Laconia*'s route far offshore, reduced but never completely eliminated the possibility of running into a U-boat looking for a ship to sink.

U-BOAT 156 AND COMMANDER HARTENSTEIN

In U-156, Commander Werner Hartenstein departed the U-boat pens in Lorient, France, and headed south toward Africa. He left about two weeks before the *Laconia* steamed away from Cape Town. He had received his orders: hunt and sink enemy ships off the coast of west Africa. It would be a memorable eighty-nine-day voyage.

On August 26 Hartenstein's crew spotted a ship. Not long after midnight U-156 submerged so it could not be spotted in the bright moonlight. The commander ordered two torpedoes fired simultaneously at the steamer. Both found their mark. Giant plumes of water shot into the air as the torpedoes tore into the ship. The *Clan Macwhirter*, a 5,941-ton merchant ship from Glasgow, Scotland, sank in ten minutes without broadcasting a distress signal. Eleven men perished from its crew of eighty-five. Hartenstein, peering through the U-boat's periscope, watched the ship go down. Then he ordered the U-156 to continue its patrol and locate another ship.

Part II

LACONIA TORPEDOED

TORPEDOES IN THE NIGHT

LACONIA AND COMMANDER HARTENSTEIN ON U-BOAT 156

September 12, 1942

LACONIA RAN UNDER STRICT WARTIME RULES AGAINST transmitting radio signals, in hopes the ship could sneak past the enemy without being detected. The ship steered a zigzag course to make it more difficult for a submarine to track. Guards were stationed on deck with binoculars to watch for any signs of enemy submarines or vessels.

As the ship headed north off the coast of Africa, Captain Sharp began sleeping in *Laconia*'s map room and taking his meals on the bridge. He had guided the ship safely for thousands of miles. Now, on the final leg of the journey, he wanted to be extra careful and near his senior officers.

The passengers, however, showed little concern. They fell into predictable habits of socializing over card games and strolling in small groups on the deck in the cool nighttime air. Often, they left their life belts in their staterooms.

Lieutenant Colonel Baldwin focused on the prisoners. He organized them into groups and had their living quarters scrubbed and sanitized. Their exercise time on deck was extended to an hour daily. "It is no exaggeration," said Baldwin, "that when I took over conditions were appalling. Apart from the filthy state of the holds there was no organization or discipline among the prisoners. All were on bread and water under a collective punishment for contraband smoking materials. But I got it canceled the same day and the prisoners had a really good meal that evening. The effect was astonishing."

But the health and hygiene of the prisoners were not Baldwin's only responsibilities. In a meeting with the officer in charge of the prisoners he was told that in the event of an emergency, they should be kept in the lower holds until a superior officer ordered them released. That part of Baldwin's responsibility would prove most challenging.

Captain Sharp continued to keep *Laconia* farther offshore—about six hundred miles—than he would have done in peacetime to hopefully avoid U-boats patrolling the coast. But it wasn't far enough.

U-156 slowly traveled on the ocean's surface, its gray hull almost impossible to distinguish from the sea. A lookout, standing on the conning tower in the center of the sub, spotted *Laconia* far off in the distance.

"Smoke cloud in sight... steamer on WNW course" was the first notation in the submarine's log midmorning on September 12, 1942. U-156 followed the ship from a safe distance for several hours. "Determined that steamer runs at 14 knots zigzagging.... Description: old passenger-freighter from 1905, estimated 7,000 GRT [gross registered tonnage]."

Commander Hartenstein was anxious to sink the ship, but he followed the U-boat commander's rules: keep the ship on the horizon, its funnels barely in sight, and plan for an attack under cover of darkness.

A daytime approach might allow a lookout on the vessel to spot the sub, giving the ship enough time to make an escape and radio for help.

Unaware of the threat lurking in the distance, the *Laconia*'s passengers were preparing for a fun Saturday evening. After dinner, couples looked forward to drinks and dancing while young sailors and soldiers played cards.

Ena Stoneman was ironing her husband George's pants while their young daughter, June, read a book on her bunk in their stateroom. The adults were going to a dance for Royal Air Force members.

Suddenly the ship shuddered and everything went black.

Ena was sure that the iron had caused an electrical malfunction. "George, I've fused the lights," she said. But the sound of rushing water followed. Without a moment's delay—and not stopping to put his pants on—George Stoneman scooped up his daughter and grabbed his wife's hand. They dashed through narrow hallways where the lights flickered, up one set of stairs after another, toward their lifeboat station on an upper deck.

The U-boat's torpedoes had hit near the center of *Laconia* after a three-minute run through the water. Hartenstein watched for the ship's reaction from about a mile and a quarter away, noting that it took the torpedoes longer than expected to hit their target.

"Firing range considerably underestimated. Therefore the steamer must be substantially larger," the submarine's log notes. "Steamer stopped. Puts out boats. Settles by the bow." The sub was "holding in position, downwind . . . waiting for sinking."

ESCAPE

LACONIA AND JIM MCLOUGHLIN

September 12

THERE WERE 1,793 ITALIAN PRISONERS OF WAR IN THE *Laconia*'s holds before the submarine attacked, but no one could estimate how many were killed outright by the two torpedoes that ripped through the hull. Estimates put the immediate death toll near five hundred.

"The ship was torpedoed in No. 1 and No. 4 holds, both of which were full of prisoners," recalled Lieutenant Colonel Baldwin. He raced down to the holds and saw that casualties were heavy. Prisoners were terrified, and they reached through cages trying to grab Baldwin, who used the butt of his gun to bat their hands away.

After working with the prisoners to improve their conditions, Baldwin now had to enforce rules laid down by his superiors: None of the prisoners were allowed out of the holds until the British civilians, officers, soldiers, and sailors had secured their places in lifeboats. That meant keeping them locked in the cages as the ship leaned to one side.

As the *Laconia* filled with water, the men screamed and strained against the bars. The prisoners were petrified by the certainty that the ship was sinking. Their Polish guards were told to attach bayonets to their guns and wait for ammunition to use if necessary.

Regardless of the force shown by their guards, the desperate prisoners fought to break free of the cages. Their guards, mostly young men, watched in horror as the Italians tore at the bars and each other.

Soon the bars were ripped away by the stress of hundreds of prisoners pushing and pulling on them. The guards deserted their posts, running for their lives. By now the ship was listing steeply toward the starboard (right) side, close to capsizing.

"People were trampled on and killed while the

Polish guards were running down the corridor, keeping their distance," recalled prisoner Bruno Beltrami.

Baldwin himself retreated to a place where he might forcibly hold the prisoners back with his gun to keep them from the lifeboat decks. But even the threat of bullets wasn't enough to stop throngs of men crazed by the thought of drowning. Some escaped the lower holds by squeezing through a series of air ducts to avoid the guards.

With help from other military officers Baldwin held the prisoners at bay so they could not reach the boat decks. Baldwin shouted to a superior officer for approval to release the prisoners, but got no answer. So Baldwin continued to keep the desperate Italians from escaping. He was worried that if the prisoners got to the boat deck, they would rush the lifeboats, making it more difficult for women and children to board.

Some prisoners managed to get past the guards and jumped into the lifeboats still being lowered. Others leaped into the sea and tried to climb aboard lifeboats, sometimes overturning them in their desperate effort to survive. Baldwin later testified that after about an hour, when the ship went over completely on its side, he released the prisoners. He jumped into the sea along with them. A vessel of the *Laconia*'s size creates suction when it submerges, pulling anything nearby underwater with it, and as the ship sank, Baldwin was sucked downward.

After what seemed like an eternity, Baldwin popped back to the ocean's surface. He gasped for air, got his bearings, and tried to save himself and others. Baldwin helped anyone around him—British, Italian, or Polish—climb onto floating wreckage. After two hours in the water he spotted a lifeboat in the gloom, and swam to it. A Polish guard and an Italian prisoner of war helped him inside.

Baldwin's concern that the Italian POWs could overwhelm the lifeboats arose because the *Laconia* did not carry enough boats to accommodate everyone on the ship. There were only thirty-two, most made from wood and thirty feet in length, with a capacity of about sixty people each. That meant only nineteen hundred passengers could get away in the boats, if all were seaworthy. Other people would have to use the forty or so rafts also on board.

Under optimal conditions and with plenty of time, about two-thirds of the passengers could evacuate securely in the lifeboats. But in the chaos and turmoil after the attack, even that was impossible. The ship's sudden sharp lean had rendered many of the boats unusable and increased the time it took to launch the others—time that was rapidly slipping away. It was especially difficult for families to stay together and for parents to keep track of their children.

Royal Navy Able Seaman Jim McLoughlin was visiting an acquaintance in the lower decks of the ship when the torpedoes hit. The twenty-year-old sailor was thrown against bulkheads and disoriented by the explosions. Despite being dazed, he knew that he must get to his station, the gun on the stern, as quickly as possible. Getting there wasn't easy.

"I felt like I'd been punched in the head by a powerful fist of sound," he later wrote. The concussion of the impact amid the metal walls of the inner ship made his brain feel like putty. Jim was in the cramped and crowded portion of the ship reserved for lower-ranking troops, many of whom did not know how to react. He found himself in a dark passageway with hundreds of panicked men yelling and stampeding blindly for an exit.

"Bloody Jerries!" some shouted, using the common nickname for Germans. Others prayed aloud or cried out for friends they couldn't find in the tumult. One *Laconia* sailor found that he was able to calm some of the frantic people by calling out, "Steady now, steady!" The phrase, often used on skittish horses, reminded the passengers to keep calm and move efficiently toward the exits.

Jim McLoughlin feared he'd never make it out of the ship alive. The ship might sink before people had an opportunity to jump off and swim away. "Everyone was pushing and shoving and trampling in the darkness, trying to reach the staircase," Jim said.

The force of the torpedo had blown away one stairway he needed to reach the lifeboat deck. Fortunately a wire-and-wood ladder was hanging on the wall where the stairs used to be, and the young sailor managed to climb above the fray.

Out on deck Jim dodged items that were sliding to the starboard side, where the deck was almost touching the ocean. People were screaming. Some tried to scramble to the high side as others plunged into the ocean. "There were no deck lights at all so it was a maelstrom of noise and frantic shapes rushing and stumbling," he remembered.

Jim and two others realized the ship's gun was useless given the deck's odd angle. The gun pointed crazily at the sky. Below, the sailors could see the small glowing lights of the ship's lifeboats being launched. The darkened and disabled *Laconia* appeared to be bleeding its human cargo into the ocean.

Abandoning the gun, Jim slid along the deck to the low side of the ship, where it leaned steeply above the water. The water seemed very far away. He grabbed a rope attached to the railing and went down the side. Then he swam as hard as he could to distance himself from the ship before it slipped below the surface. The distance would protect him from the underwater explosions as the increasing ocean pressure blew out the sinking ship's enormous boilers and bulkheads.

Jim reached a lifeboat and climbed in, but soon realized it was rapidly filling with water and nobody was doing anything about it. He leaped out and kept swimming, searching for a safe vessel. He looked back at the ship.

He was awestruck by the sight of the *Laconia*'s final moments. Its propellers emerged from the water as the stern stood nearly vertical, with the bow underwater. Then in slow motion the ship disappeared. It was approximately 9:20 p.m. on September 12, just a little over an hour after the torpedoes had struck.

The *Laconia* had been a major part of Jim's childhood in the port city of Liverpool. His father had worked as a steward on the once-majestic ocean liner. Now he felt despair witnessing its demise. It seemed unreal, as if he were asleep and having a terrible nightmare. But the cold water felt all too real, and he began stroking again, hoping to find a raft or an undamaged lifeboat to keep him alive.

Captain Sharp stayed on the *Laconia*'s bridge. Damage to the ship's internal communications prevented the bridge from issuing the order to abandon ship, but it was unnecessary as the passengers knew they had to escape quickly. The ship leaned to one side almost as soon as the torpedoes hit, and even nonsailors knew it could sink at any moment.

Senior Third Officer Thomas Buckingham put the

ship's secret codes and log books in specially weighted bags and dropped them into the sea to keep them from the Germans. Once that was done, he set off for the radio room, running down flights of stairs against the rising tide of fleeing passengers. *Laconia*'s radio operators confirmed that distress signals SSS, indicating a submarine attack, were being transmitted, but they weren't confident anyone could hear them given the ship's distance from land and weak transmission.

Panic rose in Buckingham's throat. He returned to the bridge and reported that the ship's desperate SSS message was being sent.

"Abandon ship," Sharp ordered. As Buckingham and the other officers left the bridge, they did not expect the captain to join them. There was no question that Captain Sharp would remain at the helm as the ship sank, the black water pushing into his lungs and dragging him to the seafloor with *Laconia*'s wreckage.

Chapter 4

INTO THE OCEAN

CLAUDE PARR, MOLLY DAVIDSON,
DORIS HAWKINS, AND TONY LARGE

Night of September 12 and early morning, September 13

As soon as the torpedoes struck, *Laconia* sailor Claude Parr rushed up four flights of slanting stairs, pushing through chaos, to reach boat deck A. His job was to launch the lifeboats. Half the boats hung above the deck by small cranes called davits, and half were fastened to the deck in cradles below. The torpedoes' impact had slammed some boats into the ship's steel structure; others had fallen, cracking wooden ribs and puncturing hulls.

During normal days at sea the captain would sound the horn and call "To the lifeboats!" over a loudspeaker, rousing all the passengers and crew to their assigned lifeboat stations. Claude had responded to these random drills night and day until his actions were automatic. Now he was thankful because he was able to push the pandemonium and uncertainty out of his mind and do his job.

With each boat suspended by davits, Claude and the other sailors would attach special launch lines and lower the vessel to the deck for passengers to scramble aboard. Then Claude and his mates would slowly ease the boat downward until it reached the water. After passengers unhooked the launch lines, sailors pulled them up and attached them to another lifeboat. It was a slow, painstaking process that frustrated frightened passengers who wanted to evacuate as quickly as possible.

Launching lifeboats did not always go as planned. Desperate to escape, people rushed and overfilled the boats. As soon as the boat reached the water, it capsized, tossing passengers into the cold sea. Sometimes damaged boats were lowered, only to fill with water and sink. Often, in the haste to lower boats, the launching lines weren't secure. This caused some boats and their occupants to plummet into the sea from the upper decks, hitting the water with a sickening whack. Sharks and barracudas were attracted to the commotion.

As *Laconia*'s mortal wound worsened and water poured through the holes in its starboard side, the ship leaned over, making launching lifeboats even more difficult. During the hour it took for the ship to sink, many lifeboats on Claude's side of the ship were hanging too far from the lower deck for people to reach them and get aboard. These boats had to be lowered all the way to the water while passengers climbed down swaying rope ladders to get in them. On the other side of the ship, the high angle of *Laconia*'s top deck quickly made it impossible to lower boats because they were pinned against the side of the ship.

Claude and his crew launched as many boats as they could, fighting the urge to abandon their station and jump into the sea. *Laconia* was beginning to lurch closer to sinking, making terrible noises of metal bending and interior spaces being crushed by the pressure of the water. When their final boat was lowered, Claude and his crew climbed down a rope ladder, expecting to find the lifeboat waiting for them at the bottom—but there was none.

Claude scrambled back up the ladder to locate another boat, but the *Laconia* was clearly about to slide beneath the surface. He crawled to the high side of the ship, climbed over the rail, and looked down at the sloping hull. With no choice but to let go, he slid down the rough, barnacle-encrusted surface of the hull, feeling the shells cut into his skin before splashing into the water.

It took hours for Claude to find a lifeboat in the dark. The dead bodies floating in the sea made him wonder: *Had they fallen asleep and put their faces in the water? Had they been attacked by sharks?* Fear motivated him to keep swimming. When he finally found a boat, he clung on the side until daybreak, petrified that he might fall asleep and drown. A man hanging on next to him during the night was gone in the morning.

During the first rays of sunrise Claude felt arms reach over the side and pull him into the boat.

Nineteen-year-old Molly Davidson's escape from the *Laconia* was just as harrowing as Claude's. When the torpedoes hit, she and her mother were knocked completely out of their chairs in the ship's dining room. Decorative pillars crashed to the floor and furniture overturned.

Molly and her mother immediately headed for the lifeboat stations. It wasn't easy. The ship was leaning toward its punctured side, and the women could only move along the deck by walking with one foot on the floor and one foot on the wall. Both were dressed for a dance rather than an evacuation, Molly in a yellow dress and her mother in a silk dress and high heels.

The noise and bedlam of people running for their lives didn't particularly alarm Molly. She was on her way home from a year in Malta, an island in the Mediterranean Sea, where her father was stationed with the British military. Air raids had been a daily event there. The young woman responded to the order to abandon ship with a no-nonsense purpose—until her escape went horribly wrong.

Molly and her mother approached their assigned lifeboat station, holding tightly to the outer rails lining the deck. But the angle was making it difficult to walk. Suddenly Molly's grip failed and she felt herself skidding toward the low side of the deck. Ahead of her was a hatch blown open by the force of the torpedo.

Her heart raced. She couldn't stop and would fall through this gaping hole into the bowels of the ship. The torpedoes had exploded near the engines and fuel supply, and fires were burning below. The fate looming before her was terrifying.

"There was an awful red glow and steam coming out of it," she said. "But I came up against the edge, which stopped me, and I was left peering into this awful cauldron of hell."

She was able to crawl back to her mother's side. Then they found family friend Major H. E. Creedon, who helped them to the railing where they expected to find a lifeboat waiting. Instead, rope ladders were hanging from the ship to the black sea below.

Major Creedon pushed the Davidsons toward the rail, shouting for them to grab the rope and descend. Molly went first, climbing over the railing. Dangling in midair on the swinging, swaying ladder, she was terrified of falling off. She had to swallow her fear and start moving, rung by rung, toward the black water below.

Molly was fortunate that her ladder ended in a lifeboat, where hands reached out to pull her down to safety. Others leaving the ship were not as lucky.

Many fell into the sea. If they were close to a lifeboat, and they identified themselves as British, they were pulled inside. But if they were Italian POWs they were pushed back into the water as the British held the boats for themselves.

When Molly sat up in her lifeboat, she quickly realized her mother, who was supposed to be coming down the ladder after her, did not end up in the same boat. In fact, it would be days before she knew if her mother was alive or dead.

There was no time for Molly to search for her mother or to cry about the situation because her help was needed in the lifeboat. A man was pulled out of the water with a bloody leg, the result of a barracuda or shark attack. Molly helped to stop the bleeding and dress the man's wound, but knew that if he didn't get real medical help soon, he might die of infection. When she looked down, she realized her yellow dress was smeared with his blood.

The frantic urge to escape the *Laconia* was the same for everyone experiencing the confusion created by tilting decks, flickering lights, and silenced engines. Moments before the first torpedo hit at 8:10 p.m., thirty-one-year-old nurse Doris Hawkins had checked on an ill friend, Lady Grizel Wolfe-Murray, whose room was across the hall from her own. After talking with Lady Grizel, Doris entered her own cabin to check on the fourteen-month-old baby in her care, Sally Readman. The child was asleep in her bed, with emergency supplies of powdered milk, clothing, and blankets bundled at her side.

"I was there about two minutes when the first torpedo struck us," Doris said. "It was the most sickening sensation—the whole ship shivered and stood still, and the air was filled with the smell of explosives."

Doris scooped up the baby and the emergency kit. Then the second torpedo strike threw them across the hall. Without hesitation Doris followed Lady Grizel through dark corridors and over broken paneling and splintered doors to the lifeboat deck. There they discovered their assigned boat had been destroyed.

Royal Air Force Squadron Leader H. R. K. Wells offered to help the anxious women. He escorted them through chaotic crowds to find an alternative lifeboat. Most boats were overfilled as they were lowered into the water. Another navy officer took action to help. He grabbed the baby from Doris's arms, tucked her inside the back of his coat, and tied a blanket around his waist to keep her from slipping out. Then he stepped over the side onto a swinging rope ladder and motioned the women to follow. At the bottom a crowded lifeboat bobbed in the water.

"Grizel and I climbed down somehow and found ourselves on top of the arms and legs of a panic-stricken mass of humanity," Doris said. "The life-boat was rapidly filling with water and at the same time crashing against the ship's side. Just as Sally was passed over to me the boat filled completely and capsized, and the sweet darling was flung away from me and I lost her."

Without a moment to grieve the loss of the child, Doris found herself among dozens of Italians struggling in the water, crying out for help, and drowning.

Denied access to lifeboats, many of the Italians clung to the sides of any floating raft, debris, or vessel they could find. Their thin bodies offered little strength for swimming or defense against hypothermia, which made it very challenging to swim even short distances. One grabbed Doris around the neck, dragging her underwater until she kicked him away. Another man did the same just as she was able to grab a floating board. Like before, she kicked furiously until he let go.

Finally, Doris floated close to a raft, which several Italian men helped her climb onto. Catching her breath, she slumped on the raft, picking her head up just in time to see a sad and eerie sight. The *Laconia*, its propeller now high in the air, slipped below the surface, hissing and making the water boil. Then, the ship's final explosions sent shock waves through the water. Doris felt the raft rise, and her stomach tensed. A sickening trepidation swept over her from fear of being capsized and plunged back into the dark, agitated sea. Then the raft settled in the water, and the nurse breathed a sigh of relief. She could only hope someone found the baby, but knew it was unlikely.

Getting to a lifeboat or raft was not a guarantee that one would survive. *Laconia* castaways were approximately six hundred miles from land. Survivors could only hope that the ship's distress signals were heard by someone with the ability to mount a search and rescue. Those shivering in lifeboats experienced a combination of despair over their predicament and hope for rescue as they struggled to make sense of what was happening.

Royal Navy Lieutenant L. J. Tillie instructed the Italians to get on one raft and British survivors on another. Then everyone spent hours vomiting due to the mixture of oil and seawater swallowed. Most recovered but not all.

"Tillie appeared to be in splendid form," Doris later wrote. "He cheered us with assurances of rescue on the morrow and leading us in community singing until, suddenly, he became quiet. I was suspicious and he changed places with Squadron Leader Wells. I then noticed that his right shirt sleeve was soaked with blood. He had been wounded on the ship. We could not stop the hemorrhage, and after about two hours he died."

Those fortunate enough to be on the overcrowded lifeboats spent a tense and worry-filled night, shivering from the cold and dazed.

Many of the boats took on water because their wooden planks had dried out and shrunk as they hung outside the *Laconia*, leaving gaps where water flowed in. Others were missing necessary bungs, or plugs. This allowed an inflow of seawater that required constant bailing around the crowded legs and feet of the throngs on board. Some boats were so crowded that there was no space for anyone to sit, making the boat unstable. Capsizing was a constant threat.

Although the situation was difficult inside the leaky and overfilled boats, other unlucky souls, including the majority of the Italians, were unable to climb aboard a boat at all. These poor men clung to anything they could find. They clustered around lifeboats, hoping that their numbers would discourage sharks from attacking. In some cases, British men used hatchets and bayonets to prevent Italians from climbing inside.

"It was a long, dark, and uncomfortable night," said Tony Large. His lifeboat filled with water again and again until its occupants were able to plug the drain hole with a wedge whittled from a piece of debris. The water temperature was approximately 75 degrees Fahrenheit, and the nighttime air temperature was in the lower 60s. Wet clothing only added to their misery and the chill. “It was a relief to occupy ourselves by exercising, either by rowing or by joining in the bailing, which went on almost continuously from the time of the boat’s launch.”

He thought about Captain Sharp going down with his ship. Sharp had recently dined at Tony’s parents’ home in Durban, sharing after-dinner cigars with Tony’s father, a longtime friend. Sharp’s death was a weight nineteen-year-old Tony would bear alone, along with many other tragic moments, until he saw his family again.

U-boat 156’s engine hummed near Tony’s lifeboat during the night. It cruised the surface, using its searchlight to sweep the scene of destruction and carnage.

Survivors warily watched the vessel’s conning tower rise above the wreckage, a terrifying sight. They wondered whether the wartime stories told about German submarine crews slaughtering shipwreck survivors might be true. (This was a war myth. German U-boat men had a code of conduct, and they did not kill survivors. There was only one incident in the war where a German U-boat commander did not follow this code.)

"Although the U-boat approached within twenty or thirty yards of us, no verbal challenge was offered us while we cringed and waited for the machine gun fire. We had no real idea what her captain was about. If he was looking for officers of senior rank to take prisoner, he never studied our particular boat. Perhaps, we thought, he was simply inspecting the work of his triumph," said Large.

When dawn broke on the scene of destruction, survivors saw a widening oil slick with wreckage stretching to the horizon. They were horrified to witness hundreds of drowning victims floating in the water, some corpses disfigured by sharks or barracudas. In lifeboats and on rafts, survivors stared into the distance, shivering, many still trying to account for friends or family members. Mingled among the British and in groups on their own rafts, the Italian prisoners became aware of how many hundreds of their own were lost.

British, Italians, and Poles alike sank into utter despair.

Then they saw something so surprising, they could scarcely believe their eyes. The German U-boat was coming at them, and on its deck were dozens of the Italians and even some of the British survivors from the *Laconia*.

The submarine crew was scooping survivors out of the water.

ABOARD U-156

COMMANDER HARTENSTEIN ON U-BOAT 156

Night of September 12 and early morning, September 13

WHEN AN ANNOUNCEMENT FROM THE SUBMARINE'S control room said the torpedoes hit the *Laconia*, the German crewmen on U-156 cheered. Because the submariners were often at sea in foul living conditions for weeks without the satisfaction of firing at a single ship, sinking an enemy vessel was a monumental event that each crew member took pride in.

Commander Hartenstein initially thought the ship was a small- to medium-size passenger freighter, and an old one because of the black smoke belching from its smokestack.

Within minutes of the torpedoes hitting the ship, the radiomen on the submarine listened intently to the distress signals sent by *Laconia*, relaying the information to their submarine commander. Hartenstein told them to jam the signals by transmitting from their own radios on the same frequency. This was a common tactic that delayed any rescue ships or planes.

The ship's SSS distress signal identified it as the *Laconia*, a Cunard White Star Line passenger ship. It was not a small ship, but three times the size that Hartenstein first thought! It was a significant prize for the commander and his crew, a victory that the German naval officers in occupied Paris would be proud of. This event would elevate Hartenstein's total tonnage sunk to more than 100,000 GRT, making him one of the German navy's elite submarine commanders.

Hartenstein ordered his crew to keep the submarine in its position. There he could still witness the aftermath of the attack and perhaps move in closer should he decide to take one of the *Laconia* officers prisoner.

Hartenstein and a handful of his officers stood on its exposed conning tower to watch the activity around the *Laconia* through their binoculars. From a mile away they saw emergency lights flicker, illuminating the outline of the ship, which had stopped moving. They observed that the *Laconia* was beginning to settle, meaning that the ship was visibly sinking, if slowly. Within minutes lifeboats were being launched, lowered to the water from the upper deck, each lit by a tiny lantern.

Flotsam of all sorts spewed from the wreck as it leaned to one side: boxes, cargo, even furniture tumbled into the water. People were jumping from the upper decks into the dark sea to escape. Thin rafts were pushed off the upper decks to provide flotation for those in the water.

U-156 slowly crept closer to the wreckage.

When U-156 entered the field of floating debris left by the massive ship, a crewman on the conning tower used a searchlight to look for the ship's officers among the lifeboats. It was common practice to interrogate and even take officers hostage. But instead of zeroing in on the brass buttons or white uniforms of officers, the submarine lookouts saw thin, barely clothed, terrified men float into view.

Crying "*Aiuto! Aiuto!*" (*Help! Help!*), the Italian prisoners near the U-boat desperately sought shelter from the bites of barracudas and sharks that lurked beneath the surface. Most Italians had been left to fend for themselves in the sea.

Hartenstein ordered his crew to pull a few of the men onto the deck of the U-boat to determine what was going on aboard the *Laconia*. When he understood that more than fifteen hundred of the German allies were locked in prison cages when the ship was struck, something unusual happened.

The battle-hardened submarine commander decided to save those he could from an awful fate in the ocean. Hartenstein knew that such a rescue was dangerous. If enemy planes or ships heard the *Laconia*'s distress signal they might attack his submarine should he stay near the wreck. His superior officers in the German navy might be angry with him. Yet he followed his moral compass.

"During a circle to windward Italian cries for help are heard," the U-156 log notes. "People fished out:

Italian prisoners of war from North Africa. Steamer reportedly had 1200–1800 on board."

Soon his crew had a new mission, pulling overloaded lifeboats alongside the submarine. The U-156 crew also repaired leaking lifeboats and gave survivors small amounts of food and water. Those who clearly needed medical assistance—whether British or Italian—were brought aboard the sub and taken below to be tended by a medic. Some British women and children were also brought on board.

"Steamer has sunk," the log notes. "Survivors taken on board. Shortly after sinking a heavy underwater detonation similar to a depth charge. A steamer is detected on short wave nearby."

Hartenstein's log was updated each time new information was learned from the Italians. "According to Italian statements, the British closed the watertight compartments to the living quarters of the prisoners after the hits and attempts by the Italians to board the lifeboats were repulsed at gunpoint."

It was clear that the submarine could not easily break away from the task of aiding those in peril. There were ninety refugees aboard the submarine, and the surprising presence of women and children created a particular challenge. They were too far from land to survive in lifeboats, even if there was space for everyone fleeing the wreck. Too many were clinging to flimsy rafts and scores had already died, either victims of shark attacks, drowning, or from injuries sustained in the sinking.

Crewmen from U-156 searched their personal belongings to find items of clothing for the shivering Italians huddled on the deck of the submarine. The crew's cook prepared vats of coffee and soup from the rations available, sending sailors up the conning tower with cups of steaming liquid to soothe the refugees. The deck of the submarine was teeming with people.

Hartenstein's log entries painted a picture of desperation. "Hundreds from shipwreck are floating with only life preservers," he noted. It might have been the first time he and his crew were confronted with the awful reality of their role in the war. Seeing the dead and wounded up close no longer allowed the crew to maintain the detached perspective that submarines were tools that reduced the number of enemy ships. They had to witness the fact that they caused pain and suffering to other human beings.

At 1:25 a.m. he radioed his superiors to inform them about rescuing the survivors. While German navy leaders turned a blind eye to submarine commanders giving shipwrecked sailors water and directions to land, pulling them aboard the vessel was unheard of. There was no way to know if Admiral Karl Dönitz would support Hartenstein's decision or command him to immediately end all rescue operations.

Hartenstein's message provided only the barest information.

"Sunk British Laconia—unfortunately with 1,500 Italian prisoners, 90 rescued so far."

The situation created turmoil in the highest levels of the German navy as word of Hartenstein's actions spread among those in its Paris headquarters.

Within three hours, Hartenstein had a positive response from the officer in charge of submarines, Dönitz. The admiral quickly ordered other submarines to assist Hartenstein including a code for the location: "Proceed immediately to Hartenstein in naval square FF7721 at high speed."

Dönitz then conferred with his colleagues, who

discouraged the decision to save people. It was too late, as the admiral had approved Hartenstein's actions before command staff in Berlin weighed in. The wheels were in motion and could not be stopped.

HARTENSTEIN'S CALL FOR HELP

COMMANDER HARTENSTEIN ON U-BOAT 156 AND ADMIRAL DÖNITZ

September 13

An assistant to the Führer, Adolf Hitler, called Dönitz to express Hitler's displeasure and deep concern about the rescue operation, but Dönitz held his ground. "I cannot throw these people into the water now," he said to his staff.

Still, Dönitz frequently cautioned Hartenstein to put the lives of his crew and the safety of his U-boat above the desire to save the lives of those shipwrecked.

Hartenstein and Dönitz knew that the overloaded submarine, sitting on the surface of the ocean, was a prime target for enemy aircraft. They had to find a solution to the problem in a way that didn't jeopardize the Axis alliance or destroy morale on the submarine.

The short-term situation facing Hartenstein was dire.

"Have aboard 193 men including 23 British," he told Dönitz. "Hundreds of shipwrecked are afloat with life jackets. Suggest diplomatic neutralization of the area." He added that radio monitoring indicated a ship was nearby.

He hoped that the unseen ship they had heard on the radio would come to the aid of the refugees and relieve him of the task.

Commander Hartenstein tested his submarine to ensure they could still maneuver properly with the weight of so many people aboard. The U-boats of that size generally operated with a crew of fifty-two, and even then the men were housed tightly, eating in shifts and sharing bunks. Adding nearly two hundred more bodies invited disaster: Would the sub be too heavy to resurface when necessary? What might happen to the oxygen levels if an aircraft's barrage of bombs pinned them underwater? Or worse, what if the bombs damaged the submarine's crucial bank of batteries, which allowed the craft to navigate while submerged? Noxious gases might be created. Crew members were equipped with breathing devices for such emergencies but not the passengers. Many of the survivors were injured, and if the U-boat submerged, they would not fare well.

Emboldened by Dönitz's support—or at least in the absence of an order to abandon the rescue effort—Hartenstein made a decision to expand U-156's potential lifesaving circle. The commander would flout wartime convention by asking others—from any country—to help him with the rescue efforts. Before receiving approval from Dönitz, he decided to seek any assistance he could from anyone who was nearby. He ordered a general message repeated on open radio channels in English, including U-156's location. It was a most dangerous gamble, but he felt he had to try.

"If any ship will assist the shipwrecked *Laconia* crew, I will not attack her, providing I am not attacked by ship or air force. I picked up 193 men. German submarine," said the message that Hartenstein dictated to his radioman at 4:00 a.m. on September 13, the morning after the sinking. It was sent on open channels that any ship in the area could hear.

The message was transmitted several times over frequencies often used for emergency signals.

Despite being hundreds of miles from the African coast, Hartenstein knew it was likely that the message would be picked up by British posts. And that is exactly what happened. The British military post at Freetown listened to Hartenstein's message. It's probable they also heard the ship's original distress signal but were wary of a potential trick by the German submarine to lure rescue ships close enough to attack. Rescue ships were sent, but they were warned to be extra careful and to have scouts on board continually scanning the seas for U-boats.

Admiral Dönitz was thoroughly uncomfortable with the situation but did not disagree with the sub commander's decisions. He warned Hartenstein and the other submarines rushing to the scene to be ready to submerge to evade the enemy at any time. And he added that an Italian submarine, the *Cappellini*, would also be on its way.

Dönitz continued to communicate with the U-boats he had ordered to assist Hartenstein, at first instructing them to take the surviving Italians to Bingerville in French West Africa.

The two submarines, the same long-range model IXC as U-156, were commanded by men with lots of experience: Erich Würdemann in U-506 and Harro Schacht in U-507. They were highly skilled commanders who had torpedoed many ships along the East Coast of the United States and in the Gulf of Mexico. The subs were hundreds of miles away, though, and travel would take two days in the best of conditions. Rather than use valuable military resources like submarines to transport the survivors to land, however, the German naval command decided to ask Vichy France for assistance. (Vichy France was the government of unoccupied France, which collaborated with the Germans. When Germany attacked and overran France in 1940, the French signed a peace treaty that allowed part of the country to remain independent, if only in name. Vichy was the small city where the collaborating government was located.) Vichy French ships would go to a prearranged location not far from where *Laconia* sank to pick up survivors from the German U-boats.

Meanwhile, Hartenstein was persistent in his efforts to rescue and provide help to as many *Laconia* survivors as possible. Although he could not fit any more people on his U-boat, he rescued people in the water and put them on lifeboats.

Admiral Dönitz continued to worry about the dangers of the rescue but kept his commitment to Hartenstein. A submarine's best defense is its ability to hide underwater from attackers. With a crew of fifty-two aboard that was possible, but adding more than a hundred people to the total was unheard of. If an enemy plane flew overhead, the submarine would have to "crash dive"—escape as quickly as possible by blowing air out of its tanks and turning the electric motor on. Any sailors not operating equipment during the dive would run through the sub's narrow inner hallway to the bow. This would force the bow of the submarine to slip underwater more quickly, making the descent quicker.

During a crash dive most of the crewmen had very specific tasks: closing hatches, trimming the flaps that steered the submarine, monitoring its depth and rate of descent. With all the extra people on board it would be difficult for the crew to get to their stations quickly. Untrained passengers might get in the way. That was Dönitz's concern when he repeated his warning to Hartenstein and others. An enemy plane might be able to drop bombs on a submarine that was too full to submerge quickly.

About 10:00 p.m. on September 13, twenty-four hours after the *Laconia* had sunk, Hartenstein estimated there were about fifteen hundred survivors in twenty-two overfilled lifeboats and clinging to rafts in the water. He had picked up four hundred, distributing them among lifeboats to even out the loads and keeping the most injured or frail on the submarine. The U-boat's cook worked nonstop to produce hot food and coffee for the refugees. Crewmen shared their personal supplies of skin cream to soothe sunburn, and some chatted with the shipwrecked about their families.

Nerves frayed as dawn broke on September 14. The U-156 crew continued the exhausting process of corralling lifeboats, repairing damage if possible, and providing food and medical assistance.

More than a thousand miles away on the African coast, the Vichy French fleet in Dakar had received the Germans' request for assistance and willingly sent three ships. Even at top speed, the cruiser *Gloire* and the sloops *Annamite* and *Dumont d'Urville* would take days to arrive. Locating and collecting the survivors would be a big job, as wind and currents were spreading the lifeboats and rafts over a large area. The French ships were under strict orders to arrive only in daytime and to fly their national flag conspicuously.

Rescuing British citizens shipwrecked far at sea was a fraught situation for the French sailors, particularly those who witnessed the British attack on their fleet at Mers el Kabir, Algeria, in 1940. More than twelve hundred French sailors died there when the British government sought to prevent the French navy from collaborating with the Germans. The British mined the harbor and launched attacks on their former ally's ships. But picking up the *Laconia* survivors was not a request of the British government. The shipwreck refugees would not be treated as allies but as prisoners of war.

Now, with Vichy French ships and more subs heading to the area, everyone involved knew that the situation was dangerous. The crew of a British or American plane flying overhead would be thrilled to find so many easy targets in the water.

Chapter 7

ANOTHER U-BOAT ARRIVES

COMMANDER WÜRDEMANN AND U-506

September 12–15

The crew of U-506, commanded by Erich Würdemann, was pursuing the Swedish cargo ship *Lima* near Liberia on the African coast the night of September 12. Their first attempt to torpedo the ship failed, their weapons zipping harmlessly past their target. Würdemann, a seasoned skipper, took time to understand his crew's mistake before resuming the hunt. He discovered that the angle, or direction, set on the torpedoes when they were fired was too wide.

Upon his second attempt both torpedoes hit the

Lima. It sank within twenty minutes, and three sailors perished out of a crew of thirty-three.

There wasn't time to celebrate the crew's success however, as the message from headquarters came through to rush to Hartenstein's assistance.

The order from Admiral Dönitz to meet with Hartenstein hundreds of miles out at sea was a significant change of course for Würdemann's crew. They had been heading for Cape Town, South Africa, to attack ships moving between there and Britain. U-boats had not hunted these shipping lanes near the West African coast prior to mid-1942, but improved air defenses over the North Atlantic and East Coast of the United States had pushed them to this new area.

Admiral Dönitz had instructed Würdemann, Schacht, and Marco Revedin aboard the *Cappellini* to assist U-boat 156 in rescuing the Italian POWs. The British passengers, Dönitz felt, could be put back in lifeboats and left for Allied ships to find, but he had a duty to save the Italians.

Fuel and food were a concern to Würdemann, who calculated the miles his submarine would have to travel. He immediately reported to Dönitz that

U-506 was at location FF4160. Traveling at a high speed of thirteen knots, it would take nearly two days to reach Hartenstein.

U-boat 506 arrived at the rendezvous location on the evening of September 14, but U-boat 156 was not there. Hartenstein's sub was too busy rounding up and repairing lifeboats, aiding the injured, and feeding throngs of hungry and thirsty people. But the next day, almost three days into the rescue efforts, the two U-boats finally found each other.

They met under cloudy skies with only moderate visibility. This was the perfect weather for two U-boats in the middle of the ocean. Clouds obscured their visibility from enemy planes hunting German subs. Still, the crews were on guard. A sailor was always on the conning tower, watching the sky and scanning the horizon with binoculars.

The two giant U-boats lined up bow to stern but a good distance apart to avoid any collision that waves might cause. Würdemann's crew was surprised by how many Italians were crowded on the deck of U-156. The crews inflated a rubber raft and tied it to a line cast between the submarines. It would be filled, emptied, and refilled with human cargo many times over the next couple of hours until 132 Italians were moved from U-156 to U-506.

As soon as the new passengers were settled into U-506's tight quarters, packed under bunks and tables and lining passageways, Würdemann gave the command to test dive. It was a necessary maneuver to practice, although unheard of with nearly two hundred people on board.

The Italians watched with fascination and some fear as the German crew went about their jobs, turning cranks and issuing orders to fasten hatches, blow out tanks, and adjust the vessel's angle for an underwater course. It was at least the second time the Italians had to trust their fate to strangers on a U-boat, but they had no other choice.

Using the periscope, Würdemann and his crew searched within thirty to fifty miles of *Laconia*'s sinking for lifeboats. If they found any, they would tow them back to the wreck site and wait for the French ships that Admiral Dönitz said would come within a few days.

That afternoon the U-boat came upon four

lifeboats in which British passengers cowered. The British were unaware of the rescue operation and were afraid the Germans would slaughter them. Women and children were hidden under tarps and blankets in the center of the boat to protect them. Molly Davidson was among this group.

MOLLY
SEPTEMBER 12–16

Molly had been packed with about seventy others on one lifeboat, bobbing on the sea for four days with little fresh water and almost no food. The anticipation of rescue had dulled after so many hours of rocking and watching the gray horizon. She'd given her waterproof watch to the helmsman of the lifeboat to assist navigating the vessel in the direction of the African coast. But she knew they'd made no real progress because there were only a couple of oars. Everyone on board was weakened by thirst and hunger.

Now with the arrival of U-506, Molly didn't know what to expect.

"Do you have water?" a German sailor asked, surprising everyone with his English.

Then the sailor inquired if women or children were aboard. After a little coaxing, the dehydrated and shaky passengers accepted fresh water. Given this proof of their good intentions, Molly was among eight British women and three children to cautiously climb from the lifeboats to the deck of the U-boat. The rest of the British passengers on the four different lifeboats stayed with their boats. Using rope, German sailors tethered each boat in a long line and fastened the chain of lifeboats to the stern of the U-506. This way they would stay where the French ships could find them.

Meanwhile, Molly descended the ladder inside the submarine's conning tower. Her eyes adjusted to the dark interior, and she saw dozens of injured Italian POWs among the German crewmen. She and the other women were shown to a small alcove where a table and seats were designated for their use.

A medic checked the women and children for injuries. Crewmen left them jars of skin cream to soothe sunburn. Some sailors even approached the women to show them family photos, explaining that they had wives and children at home in Germany.

Molly told the Germans that she was traveling with her mother aboard the *Laconia* but that they'd been separated when evacuating. This elicited an interesting response. Every time U-506 approached a new lifeboat, a crewman would find Molly and take her up the ladder to the conning tower to look for her mother. Once she spotted a man she knew in a boat.

Molly called to him, "Have you seen my mother?"

The man shook his head no.

During quiet moments Molly thought of her father, leading a British military unit fighting the Germans. Unsure she'd ever see her mother again, she resolved to make her way home somehow. *Father couldn't bear to lose both of us*, she thought.

CLAUDE AND CHAOS IN THE LIFEBOAT

CLAUDE PARR

September 12–16

After being pulled into a lifeboat, Claude Parr was thankful to be alive, but he fully understood the precarious nature of his predicament. There were 104 people crammed inside a large lifeboat that was designed for eighty. Debris and carnage surrounded them. It was "a graveyard of floating bodies," Claude said, "their faces submerged in the water."

Claude's survival instinct kicked in when he realized most of the people in the vessel hadn't a clue about lifeboat safety. Claude and three other men on board were qualified to manage a lifeboat, having taken a two-day course that earned them the Board of Trade Lifeboat Certificate. The four trained sailors needed to take charge.

Their first step was to make sure the lifeboat was as stable as possible, and they moved people around. As the sun grew stronger the morning after the sinking, steam rose from everyone's wet clothing. Some people talked about trying to sail toward Africa, but others thought it best to drift, which is what they did that first full day in the lifeboat. The breeze and current carried them away from where the ship sank.

As evening approached, they felt utterly alone in the fading light. They did not see any other lifeboats nor any U-boats. To keep the boat stable in the swells, the sailors decided to row. They kept the bow pointed into the swells, and rowed slowly but steadily.

Just before darkness obscured his vision, Claude heard shouting in the water. He saw a couple of small life rafts with people clinging to them and pleading for help. But with the big lifeboat already jammed, they let the rafts drift away to an uncertain fate.

Of the more than a hundred survivors in Claude's

lifeboat, only one was a woman. In the confusion after the attack, she had become separated from her daughter, who was about ten years old. The mother had climbed into the lifeboat and desperately told a Royal Air Force man about her daughter. The brave man climbed back up the hanging ladder to try to find the young girl. Neither he nor the daughter was ever seen again. The mother suffered greatly.

After the sun set, those not rowing began shivering in the cold of this second night of their ordeal. The wind increased and so did the swells. Seawater came in over the bow, adding to their misery.

The next day, around midmorning, Claude was startled out of his cold stupor. An area of the ocean's surface a hundred yards away became turbulent. Was it a whale? A huge school of fish? Suddenly the conning tower of a U-boat broke through the surface of the sea.

Claude and the others crouched in fear.

The sub advanced. It was likely U-507, commanded by Harro Schacht.

U-boat sailors climbed out of the conning tower and stood on the sub's deck. Some held guns. One man, wearing a cap and white trousers, appeared to be the commander.

He lifted a megaphone to his mouth and shouted in English, "Do you have a captain or senior officer on board?"

"No!" hollered back the survivors.

"Do you have rations?"

"No!" was the answer.

The German commander told the castaways a ship would be coming, and he pointed in the direction they should row. Then he and his men climbed back into the sub and it moved off.

Claude and the others weren't sure what to do. This was their first contact with a U-boat. Why was their enemy pointing them toward a potential ship? Was it a trap? A cruel joke? After all, it was a U-boat that had put them in this position.

After much discussion they decided to put their trust in the U-boat commander. They hoisted their sail and rowed in the direction shown them. (Many of the lifeboats had sails, and Claude's lifeboat was one of the few where the sail was in working order.) All day they sailed, and at night they dropped the sail and used the oars to keep the bow pointed into the swells.

The wind sent a salt spray on the castaways, matting their hair and stinging their eyes and parched lips.

Another bleak dawn arose, September 15, and the survivors knew it could be days before a ship came. Perhaps no ship was even searching for them. There was only one small canister of water on board, and the survivors rationed it: a couple of tablespoons in the morning and a couple more in the evening. Food was also in short supply and consisted of some biscuits, pemmican (a pasty spread composed of dried meat and berries), and Horlick's malted milk tablets. The vessel also contained some rope and a flare.

Boredom made the hours pass slowly. The lone woman, however, was a brave one. Despite the trauma of losing her daughter, she did her best to comfort others. She tried to take their mind off their plight and distract them from the pain of their injuries. She led various quiz games to keep people occupied. The games helped, but the diversion was brief, and most could not ignore their craving for water. Claude came to have the utmost respect for the woman because she never complained.

Later that day, one of the men became belligerent. He walked down the center of the boat, pushing people aside. People shouted at him to sit down, but the man was not acting rationally. Perhaps his mental state was imbalanced because of the trauma of the sinking or the early effects of dehydration. Whatever the cause, he was a real threat to everyone's safety. His movements were so abrupt that the boat rocked dangerously from side to side, in jeopardy of capsizing.

Some men swatted him, demanding he sit down. But the crazed man only muttered, "I'm going down to the bar for a drink. I need a drink." He continued to push people aside as he walked with a purpose.

Fast action was needed before all the survivors ended up back in the sea. An officer waited for the man to pass, then with a mighty blow, hit him on the back of his head with his fist. The man tumbled to the deck, completely unconscious.

Other men quickly tied him up and stuffed him in the sail locker at the very tip of the bow.

Claude went back to rowing, and another night fell. The young man's hands were becoming increasingly raw from gripping the oar. Adding to his pain, water rations had been cut in half as officers realized their supply would soon run out. Claude, in an effort to relieve his suffering and generate enough saliva to talk, took a button off his coat and kept it in his mouth, sucking it as he rowed. But his tongue had become dry and hard, and the button did little good.

During the night the waves increased, and many of the survivors were seasick. But a few drops of rain perked everyone up. They only had a couple of miniscule containers to try to catch the water. The drops that fell into the bottom of the boat were useless because they mixed with the seawater already there. And then the raindrops stopped falling just minutes after they began.

The next morning, September 16, some men opened the sail locker to check on the man who had gone delirious. While pulling him out, they realized his body was stiff and rigid. Once he was fully out, it was clear he was dead.

The survivors were in such a state of misery with their thirst and hunger that no one even cared the man had died. Instead, they removed his clothes and gave them to people who had few. Every item of clothing, no matter how ragged, offered protection from the sun during the day and from the brutal cold at night.

Once the dead man's clothing was removed, someone said a prayer, and his body was eased overboard, where it floated away. Claude wondered who would be next.

ASCENSION ISLAND

WIDEAWAKE AIRFIELD

September 12–16

THE DEBRIS AND OIL SLICK LEFT BY *LACONIA* SPREAD across a wide swath of the ocean's surface, covering considerable miles. In it were many of the lifeboats, rafts, and individual survivors clinging to hope that a rescue ship would arrive.

The British Admiralty's West Africa Command in Freetown had picked up the *Laconia*'s SSS signal and dispatched two ships: the HMS *Corinthian*, a boarding vessel, and the merchant ship *Empire Haven*. It would take several days for them to reach the site. In that time, the lifeboats would be so spread out that the ships wouldn't be able to find them.

Wind and waves were pushing the small boats about fifteen miles a day, and some survivors had decided to row toward Africa, six hundred miles away. Only a few lifeboats were towed by U-156, which tried to keep them close to the location of the sinking so that rescue ships might find them. The waves made it difficult to spot small boats, let alone rafts, in the vast ocean, and no one knew exactly how many lifeboats to look for. Because the ship had sunk so quickly that night, there was never an accurate count of how many boats and rafts were launched. The longer it took for rescuers to arrive, the more difficult it would be to determine whether all were found.

The British West Africa Command relayed the information about the *Laconia* to Americans on Ascension Island, a spit of volcanic rock in the Atlantic Ocean midway between Africa and Brazil. The British requested that the Americans provide defensive air cover for the rescue ships.

Although the Germans were not yet aware of it, Ascension Island, once a British outpost for laying undersea communication cables, had just become host to a secret American air base, called Wideawake Field. It was named for the thousands of sooty terns, called wideawakes, that nested there. The birds were not welcome because they created a hazard for aircraft. They sometimes flew into planes' propellers and windscreens. The military tried to eradicate the birds but were unsuccessful because the terns had been migrating to the island to lay their eggs for thousands of years.

The runways were hastily constructed in ninety days by men who worked twelve-hour shifts and lived in small cinderblock buildings on the desolate island. When a U-boat sank the construction crew's supply ship earlier that summer, they briefly lived like shipwreck survivors, almost running out of food and drinking water.

In August the First Composite Squadron of the US Army Air Force arrived, commanded by Captain Robert C. Richardson III. The squadron's primary planes were P-39 Airacobra fighters and larger B-25 Mitchell bombers. These aircraft were assigned to patrol thousands of square miles of airspace and waters between Brazil to the west and North Africa to the east to ensure safe travel for Allied ships and planes. The island was becoming an important stop for US military planes. Aircraft moving from North America through Brazil to Africa and Europe often stopped at Ascension Island to refuel.

On September 15, just a month after his arrival at Wideawake Field, Captain Richardson was notified of the *Laconia* sinking by a British communications officer relaying the ship's distress signal heard by the British military in Freetown, on the African coast. Richardson assumed it meant the ship had been torpedoed that day, and he agreed to assist the British ships sent to look for survivors. Richardson flew a B-25 to search for lifeboats and wreckage.

Richardson spotted some of *Laconia*'s lifeboats and the British ships that were looking for them. The planes, however, were not equipped with radios that could communicate with the ships.

"We did what we could," Richardson said of attempts to aid the rescue of survivors. Pilots watched helplessly as rescue ships were unable to find nearby lifeboats due to high waves. "We would point to the direction of lifeboats, but the sea was too high; the freighters were too small. They would pass each other without picking anybody up." The twenty minutes that the B-25 planes were able to stay overhead proved futile.

"The second time I got out there...the lifeboats and debris had spread over a really vast area. I would say there was an oil slick that might have been 20 to 30 miles wide," he said. "People were all over the ocean; the sea was still high. The British freighters were in sight and doing absolutely no good as rescue boats. They were too small and had none of the appropriate gear. A lifeboat could go by in one trough between waves, and they would go by in the other and wouldn't see it."

Then a larger American B-24 Liberator bomber with a crew of five stopped at Wideawake Field for some engine work on its way from the United States to the Middle East. Richardson pushed to get their engine repaired. The Liberator crew was inexperienced, but he wanted them to fly over the wreckage to look for *Laconia* lifeboats and survivors. A Liberator was capable of flying longer than a B-25, making it better suited to the job of helping the rescue ships.

Now, on September 16, the third full day after *Laconia* was sunk, the Liberator flew toward the scene of the sinking. Those in lifeboats were being tested by every wave that rocked their vessels. They prayed for salvation in the form of friendly planes or rescue ships.

Part III

AMERICAN PLANE BOMBING AND AFTERMATH

Chapter 10

BOMBS FROM ABOVE

AMERICAN LIBERATOR BOMBER

September 16

LOOKING DOWN FROM THE COCKPIT OF HIS RUMbling Liberator, US Army Air Force Lieutenant James D. Harden saw a submarine on the gray surface of the Atlantic. Despite being new to submarine hunting, Harden realized it was rare to find such easy prey. The sub didn't try to evade him by submerging, nor was it shooting at his aircraft. He could sink it easily with the bombs in the belly of his plane, eliminating a deadly threat to Allied ships. Instead, he paused and began circling to get a better look.

A white flag emblazoned with a red cross—the internationally recognized symbol of a humanitarian mission that was off-limits to combat—was draped across the antiaircraft gun in front of the submarine's conning tower. The deck was crowded with people, far more than made sense under normal circumstances. Four lifeboats were being towed behind the vessel.

The scene 250 feet below Harden was a puzzle. Seeing what looked like shipwreck refugees aboard and around what appeared to be a German U-boat was completely unexpected.

Harden told his crew to take out the Aldis lamp to signal the submarine. Flashing a message in pulses of light at the vessel's conning tower, the crew of the airplane demanded to know the submarine's nationality since there was no flag visible.

On the submarine the crew scrambled to ward off the deadly threat the aircraft represented. They brought a British officer, Lieutenant Peter Medhurst, to the conning tower and instructed him to respond to the plane's signals. Medhurst complied, telling the aircrew through the blinking light that there were British personnel, women, and children aboard the submarine.

The American airmen claimed the only response

from the submarine that they understood was "German, Sir," which confused them. The pilot thought about providing first aid or survival supplies to those in the overfull lifeboats, but the crew had little to spare.

"We did circle a while to see if we could give them any assistance but we couldn't as we didn't have any supplies," Harden said. "We dropped some water jugs."

Then the Liberator left to seek advice from superior officers, flying about a hundred miles in thirty minutes to make radio contact with Wideawake Field.

"We thought they wanted help," Harden said. "We radioed to Ascension Island that they needed help."

Harden hailed the base and described the scene: the red cross flag, the lifeboats, the lack of aggression from the submarine. He requested orders, direction, any kind of guidance for proceeding. Then he waited, circling in the clouds.

Finally a voice crackled over the radio. "Sink sub at once" was the blunt message. The terse order was issued by Captain Richardson. Both Richardson and

Harden were just twenty-four years old, and they were making life-and-death decisions.

A submarine was dangerous to more than just ships in the ocean. Richardson knew that even the airfield at Ascension Island was vulnerable to a U-boat attack. A submarine's guns could blow up parked airplanes or the airfield's fuel depot. Earlier in the year Commander Werner Hartenstein had set out to do just that. In mid-February 1942 he sailed U-156 into the harbor of the Dutch island of Aruba in the Caribbean, with the intent of blowing up the island's oil refineries with the submarine's deck gun. However, the U-156 gunners had forgotten to remove a protective cap from the end of the barrel, causing the weapon to explode in their faces. Instead of destroying the refinery, the submarine torpedoed several tanker ships in the harbor and left.

When Richardson received Harden's request for orders, he consulted with his superiors. He discussed what Harden had seen with Colonel James A. Ronin and Captain Willard W. Wilson. They had to decide quickly as the aircraft was burning precious fuel in a holding pattern. The officers had been told there were no Allied submarines in the area, so they knew the sub was German. They quickly agreed that their priority was protecting ships and their air base from U-boats, despite the apparent shipwreck survivors. Richardson said he assumed U-156 was picking up the prisoners of war who had been on *Laconia*. He knew that there were also British military and civilians among *Laconia*'s passengers but was unsure if they were on the U-boat or in the lifeboats being towed.

Attacking the submarine was an opportunity for Harden and his crew in the Liberator to protect mariners and earn an air medal. Still, the crew was conflicted. Something about the mission seemed wrong. The sub crew could be playing a trick on them with the red cross flag, but if they were, why didn't they shoot while the aircraft was overhead? The lifeboats in tow and people covering the deck clearly indicated the U-boat was in a rescue operation.

Harden pondered the order. "They wired back 'sink sub at once,' just four words," the pilot recalled. "I was afraid we might hit the lifeboats, but it looked like the lesser of two evils was to sink the submarine."

The Liberator wheeled around and headed back. The scene below was unchanged, but this time the people in the lifeboats looked up in horror. Harden's bombardier, Lieutenant Edgar W. Keller, had opened the bomb-bay doors, signaling an impending attack. People on the submarine's deck started to scatter, and those in the lifeboats froze in disbelief.

BLOWN INTO THE SEA

COMMANDER HARTENSTEIN ON U-BOAT 156

TONY LARGE AND DORIS HAWKINS

September 16

As the bombs tumbled a short 250 feet from the Liberator toward Hartenstein's U-boat, people poured out of the hatch on the sub's conning tower. The British had been ordered to leave the U-boat immediately. Italian POWs inside the sub were initially allowed to stay.

Survivors on deck screamed and cowered. Sailors scrambled to cut the lines that tethered the crowded lifeboats to its stern, setting them adrift. Many *Laconia* survivors on the sub jumped into the ocean and began swimming toward the jam-packed lifeboats.

Tony Large, in the nearest lifeboat, watched in horror as the first bombs fell from the plane. He knew that many people were in mortal peril. The plane's first attempts to hit the exposed and undefended submarine fell harmlessly distant, but then it circled back for a second try.

Tony witnessed the second attempt as if in slow motion. The bombs were dropped too late to hit the submarine and cartwheeled in the sky toward the lifeboats behind it. The first bomb hit the water between the first and second vessels, and the second bomb landed just ten feet from the gunwale of the first lifeboat, blowing Tony into the air.

The young Royal Navy man felt as if a giant hammer had hit his lifeboat, sending him airborne. When he landed in the ocean, Tony was surprised to find himself unhurt. He treaded water among the wreckage with other survivors, hoping he would not be hit by another bomb.

Inside the submarine, sailors and passengers were tossed against bulkheads by the bomb's concussions. A leak of poisonous gas from the sub's batteries was detected, and Hartenstein ordered the Italian POWs overboard as well. The U-boat did not have enough gas masks for them. The crew cursed the airplane as they locked down hatches and blew out the tanks in preparation for a crash dive. Soon the big vessel was slipping below the surface, washing any remaining bodies from its deck and leaving capsized lifeboats in its wake. The men and women who had found shelter on Commander Hartenstein's sub were now left to the mercy of the ocean.

The Liberator's bombs wouldn't release from the cradle every time, but while the conning tower of the sub was still visible, the last bomb rocked it with a huge explosion. A final GP, a general-purpose bomb, was dropped in the submarine's wake, hitting a lifeboat. Clinging to an overturned lifeboat, Tony watched as the enormous U-boat was lifted by the force of the final blasts.

Nurse Doris Hawkins had been on the submarine with dozens of others, including some who were sick or injured. When the bombs began to fall, the German submarine crew hurried the passengers up the conning tower ladder and into the seething ocean. Doris and her friend, Lady Grizel Wolfe-Murray, plunged off the U-boat together. They swam with two men toward the nearest lifeboats.

Tony was helpless to assist.

The U-boat did not try to defend itself against the attack by the Liberator, Tony recalled. He was aghast at what he saw, including the weak and injured being ejected from the safety of the submarine and told to swim to already full lifeboats. He knew that many of the *Laconia* passengers didn't make it to safety.

Tony and another man righted their lifeboat, removing four dead bodies trapped inside, and attempted to bail it out. It had been severely damaged, and their efforts were unsuccessful in the choppy sea. Ballast tanks that gave the lifeboat buoyancy began floating away, and as more people climbed aboard, the impaired lifeboat capsized frequently. Already weakened by days of exposure and little sustenance, many drowned.

Doris estimated that most of the fifty British citizens taking shelter on the submarine before the bombing died in the water. She knew of only six who made it to lifeboats.

An entire lifeboat full of POWs was destroyed in the incident.

While the *Laconia*'s voyage had begun with Italian POWs outnumbering British passengers by two-to-one, just a fraction of the Italians would ever set foot on solid ground again. Yet they were the reason the German U-boat had stopped to render aid. Without the Italians, British casualties of the torpedoed *Laconia* would have been much higher.

JOSEPHINE BOARDS U-507

COMMANDER SCHACHT ON U-507

JOSEPHINE FRAME

September 16–17

Commander Würdemann and his crew heard a radio message from U-boat 156 reporting the bombing. Hartenstein was abandoning the rescue effort.

U-156's message was quickly followed by one from Admiral Dönitz that made it clear the U-boats were to be kept safe at any cost.

"The safety of the boat must not be compromised under any circumstances. Take all precautions, including cessation of rescue efforts mercilessly. Expectation of indulgence of U-boat by the enemy is incorrect."

The submarine commanders did not know the pressure Dönitz was under from his superiors, who chastised him after the bombing of U-156. The loss of a U-boat during such a hazardous rescue operation would put the admiral in bad standing with his boss, Admiral Erich Raeder, and with Hitler. Dönitz was torn, knowing that the rescue operation was nearing an end.

"After this attack on U-156 from the service point of view, it would have been correct for me to abandon all rescue work," Dönitz wrote in his memoir. "There was a very heated discussion at my headquarters during which some of my officers argued, very rightly, that any further attempts at rescue would be wholly unjustifiable. But once I had set my hand to the task I could not bring myself to abandon it and I put an end to the discussion with the words, 'I cannot put those people into the water. I shall carry on.' "

Dönitz was referring to the rescue efforts of the two U-boats that had just arrived on the scene. Having forced everyone his crew had cared for off the vessel, British and Italian alike, Hartenstein had moved off to assess and repair the damage to his U-boat. The periscopes and listening gear didn't work properly, compromising the submarine's defenses. The gas leak from the batteries was stopped.

German submarines were well equipped with technology that allowed them to desalinate ocean water for drinking, to travel at high speeds, and to search the horizon and sky through periscopes. They were, however, vulnerable to attacks that might crack the outer steel shells. A small water leak that went unfixed might lead to bigger equipment problems that could hinder maneuvering or even cause the sub to sink. Hartenstein was relieved to find no water leaks after the attack. "Miracle of German shipbuilding work," the U-156 log notes.

Headquarters remained extremely nervous about another attack. "Do not set red cross flags," a message to the U-boats warned. "In no case, at least with the English, has it offered proven protection."

A few hours later another reminder was directed to Schacht and Würdemann. "Boats must be ready to crash dive at any time and be fully capable of operating submerged. Deliver the rescued to lifeboats. Keep only Italians on board. Go to the meeting place naval square FE9695 and deliver them to the French. Beware of hostile action by aircraft."

Both Schacht and Würdemann disregarded the order to put the vulnerable women, children, and injured in lifeboats. They knew the end of the operation was near, so they took a chance and kept those people inside the subs.

Back in the lifeboats, fourteen-year-old Josephine Frame and her parents were suffering in a drifting boat packed with sixty people. She was exhausted by seasickness, dehydration, the searing sun, and the bone-chilling cold.

Their bulky life jackets, which were like two pillows, one in front and one in back strapped over the shoulders and under the arms, propped a person's head up even when sleeping. Everyone seemed to be listless and lethargic, closing their eyes to escape the reality of their dire situation. They were drifting out of sight of other lifeboats and knew nothing of their chances for rescue or survival. They were just surviving, one minute at a time.

Wearing only cotton pajamas, Josephine thought about how she'd been climbing up a ladder to her brother's bed when the first torpedo struck. She hung on to the bed rail and looked to her parents for reassurance. Then the second torpedo struck, and they were running. When the family got to the top of the grand staircase, headed for their lifeboat station, the staircase fell away behind them, still crowded with people desperate to get off the ship.

Josephine wished she had been able to take some of her belongings with her during the escape. She really wanted the tin combat helmet she was bringing home to England, but it was gone forever, sunk with the *Laconia*. Like Molly Davidson, she and her family had lived on a British military base, in Singapore, and had experienced the war firsthand. The helmet bore a scar from a Japanese machine gun's bullet, a trophy she hoped to show friends, but the *Laconia* sinking would be more significant than even that.

In the lifeboat Josephine was fortunate to have her parents with her. She was embarrassed to tell them that she needed to use the bathroom on the second day, but her father arranged for her to move toward the side of the boat and for a couple of men to hold on to her. They helped Josephine lower her body toward the water to relieve her bowels. Other men stood by with oars to fend off sharks that might be nearby.

When it was announced that rations were being reduced, everyone grumbled. It was hard to imagine surviving on less than the three tiny sips of water a day that they had been getting. Chewing the tough biscuits would be impossible with less water. Josephine worried sometimes that the anger and frustration that some people expressed about their situation would boil over into a fight that would tip the boat over. She'd already seen a similar tragedy the night of the torpedoing: another family had put one of their sons in a lifeboat that was being lowered from the upper deck and just as the boy got aboard, the rope snapped, dumping dozens of people into the ocean. She remembered the mother's screams and the feeling of despair knowing nothing could be done to save the child.

On the fourth day since the *Laconia* sinking, someone shouted that a submarine was coming toward them. It was the Italian sub *Cappellini*.

As the submarine approached, the commander appeared on the conning tower, asking in a thick accent about Italians in the boat. There were two, both badly injured. Sailors from the submarine, helped to move the two men off the lifeboat. Then the commander asked whether anyone else was hurt. Someone told him there was a baby on board in dire need of nourishment. The commander shouted down into the conning tower and soon produced a tin of milk. Then they were gone.

The lifeboat passengers were confused by the Italian submarine's appearance: Did it mean they'd be rescued? Most were consoled that someone knew they were out there, that they weren't alone. Just seeing the submarine gave them hope, something to cling to.

Hope began to fade the next afternoon until another submarine approached. This one was German, U-507, skippered by Commander Harro Schacht.

Like the Italian sub commander, the leader of U-507 spoke English. "I would like the women and children to come aboard," he said. Some people protested, but Schacht was gently persuasive. Few of the women could resist the opportunity to get out of the sun and to eat something other than hard biscuits and pemmican. Josephine, with her stepmother and brother, climbed out of the lifeboat and down the ladder inside the conning tower of U-507.

Although the submarine was already filled with Italian prisoners, the women and children were given several officers' bunks to stretch out in. Josephine was exhausted from worrying that the lifeboat would tip over, dumping her family into the shark-infested water. Yet there was a lot of activity on the U-boat, including more people descending the conning tower and crew members checking gauges. She ate some stew and quickly fell asleep.

Schacht and U-507 soon found another lifeboat drifting alone with forty-nine people aboard. Ena and George Stoneman were inside with their child, June. The women were taken aboard the U-boat while George and the other men were left in the lifeboat. Ena and June were shown a bunk near the torpedo room. A sailor handed June a chocolate bar, even holding her on his lap while she ate it and drank a cup of milk.

"In the middle of the night I woke up and saw that June was talking to the German," recalled Ena Stoneman. "He was trying to understand what she was saying. And would you believe, she was trying to tell him she was thirsty and wanted a glass of water. I helped him understand. He smiled, went off, and came back with the water. Just like any dad getting up in the middle of the night.

"When we awoke in the morning, we got a big breakfast of semolina, and some of the sailors took off their heavy socks and gave them to the children. There was quite a festive atmosphere aboard the boat. I think it was because most of the Germans had been away from home for so long and many were family men. They missed their own kids and were spoiling ours. One sailor—the one whose bunk we used—showed us a picture of his wife and children and looked at it quite longingly."

Commander Schacht interrogated Thomas Buckingham, the *Laconia*'s senior third officer, and relayed the information he learned to Dönitz. *Laconia* had eight guns on its upper decks, he reported, along with depth charges. In the eyes of the Germans, that information justified torpedoing the ship because *Laconia* was armed.

Buckingham also detailed the number of passengers and their nationalities, helping Schacht to estimate how many full lifeboats might be drifting on the wind and currents. The information Buckingham provided was valuable, so he was kept on board.

Buckingham and one other *Laconia* officer would become prisoners of war.

The U-boat continued to collect survivors in the area as it waited for the Vichy French ships to arrive at the rendezvous point for the transfer. The French would carry them to Africa. Although the transfer would end the U-boats' dangerous rescue efforts, it was still a source of concern. The Germans didn't completely trust the French, and the sentiment was mutual. Dönitz had laid down strict rules for contacting the French ships. Those included radio codes and signal lights that would prevent any misidentification or misunderstanding.

Admiral Dönitz, under pressure from his superiors and alarmed that the American bomber had attacked U-156, sent a message on September 17 to the entire U-boat fleet around the world that included the following: "Do not pick up men or take them with you. Do not worry about merchant ships' boats. Weather conditions and distance from land play no part. Have a care only for your own ship and strive only to attain your next success as soon as possible. We must be harsh in this war. The enemy began the war in order to destroy us, so nothing else matters."

Called the Laconia Order, his command was an attempt to prevent another tragedy and loss of a U-boat and its crew.

The order elevated trepidation among the U-boats on the scene. Schacht's and Würdemann's crews were on high alert. Allied bombers had flown overhead and might return or send their own submarine. The U-boats had to assume they could be attacked at any moment.

CRASH DIVE

COMMANDER WÜRDEMANN ON U-506

MOLLY DAVIDSON

September 16–17

Commander Erich Würdemann was tense and agitated. He was well aware that having surfaced U-boats just a few miles apart from one another was tempting fate. Just one enemy aircraft with enough bombs and a little luck could potentially sink all three subs. And if the enemy knew about the Italian soldiers on board, that might tempt them further. He had just heard about the air attack on Hartenstein, and the commander was getting more nervous by the minute.

Würdemann's sub was jammed with Italians and a

few British women and children, almost two hundred in total. They sat or stood in every available space, jamming hallways, officers' quarters, bunks, and even the engine room. The commander was concerned the survivors would be in the way and potentially slow his men should they need to run to their stations for a crash dive. He made sure his men were not letting their guard down, and he walked from station to station.

The Italian soldiers were all thin and hollow eyed. Some had no shirts or pants when taken on board. Many looked starved. Würdemann didn't have much food to spare but did his best, giving all the castaways soup, coffee, and small pieces of chocolate.

In the commander's war diary he wrote that the British women and children were the dependents of soldiers and colonial officials from African outposts. "They felt very comfortable on board, though an excited woman had first asked quite anxiously whether they would now be killed." He went on to write that another woman said she would find a way to get a message to Winston Churchill about "the helpful attitude of the Germans on the U-boats."

While Würdemann was glad to be of assistance to

the women and children, he knew he wasn't following orders to the exact letter. Dönitz had ordered him to keep only Italians on the sub and put the British back in lifeboats. Würdemann did not feel the time was right for such a move, but on the other hand he had recently received the Knight's Cross from Dönitz—a high honor—and he didn't want to jeopardize his good standing. So he was torn on what to do. For now he would keep the British on board while continuing to search for survivors still in the ocean.

The commander himself spent much of his time on the conning tower, scanning the skies with his binoculars for approaching aircraft along with the usual lookout. It was the right move: he heard and saw a plane approaching and immediately sounded the alarm to dive.

Molly Davidson was resting in U-506 when a commotion started. People were yelling and running down the sub's passageway. An alarm began to sound. Hatches were slammed shut.

Other survivors got tense and worried. What was happening? The Germans didn't have time to explain.

Each had a job to do, whether monitoring gauges, turning valves, or adjusting the rudders. These tasks were made more challenging by the extra bodies underfoot in every nook of the vessel.

Molly soon realized they were crash diving, and the excitement thrilled her. She was actually submerging in a submarine, something she had only heard about. Unlike others who cried or prayed aloud, she felt a thrill from all the activity around her. She even managed to laugh when a little British girl on board insisted on wearing her life jacket for the crash dive.

Molly turned a bit more serious as the boat started to descend. The steep angle of the dive surprised her.

The survivors weren't aware that Hartenstein's submarine had been bombed, but now it was happening to U-506. It was clear from the activity and tense language used by the crew that an aircraft had spotted the submarine and was trying to sink it. Fortunately the American plane had been located early enough for the sub to evade the bombs. U-506 dove before the plane was able to release its bombs and was well underwater before the explosions shook the submarine.

The sub stayed submerged for about ninety minutes until the commander determined by peering through the periscope that the danger had passed. Those on board had escaped without injury or damage, and Molly Davidson had a story to tell her friends back home. Even so, her adventure wouldn't end for months.

Later that afternoon a lookout on the conning tower sighted the mast of a large ship: the Vichy French cruiser *Gloire* with the smaller sloop *Annamite*. Molly was delighted. She incorrectly assumed she would soon be safe and free.

Part IV

WEEKS IN THE LIFEBOATS

NO ROOM TO SIT

JIM MCLOUGHLIN AND DORIS HAWKINS, LIFEBOAT #1

September 16–17

AFTER THE LIBERATOR AIRCRAFT DROPPED ITS BOMBS on Hartenstein's sub, twenty-year-old Jim McLoughlin found himself in the same lifeboat as nurse Doris Hawkins. Yes, the two were out of the chilly water, but try to imagine this scene: sixty-eight people were crammed on a thirty-foot wooden vessel.

The castaways consisted of sixty-four British men, two Polish officer cadets, and two women, Doris and Lady Grizel Wolfe-Murray. Among the British men were a handful of officers from the army, Royal Air Force, and *Laconia* crew, including the ship's twenty-six-year-old surgeon, Dr. Geoffrey Purslow. The vessel was so crowded that most survivors had to stand shoulder to shoulder.

The lifeboat rode up and down gentle waves, and despite standing on weary legs, everyone was able stay in position and not fall overboard. Jim marveled at this and thought perhaps it was because they were wedged so tightly. If the wind picked up and generated steeper waves, survivors might tumble like bowling pins, and some would land back in the water.

For now, however, there was no dangerous wind. That was certainly fortunate, because the gunwales of the lifeboat—the top edges of the vessel—were precariously close to the water due to all the human weight inside. The lack of wind was about the only thing in the survivors' favor; every other factor soon seemed to conspire against them.

On the lifeboat after the American plane attacked U-156, the air grew cold, and the survivors suffered, with sleep nearly impossible. Water sloshed around the bottom of the boat, keeping their feet wet, adding to their misery. Muffled groans of discomfort arose from many of the survivors, mixed with the occasional agonizing cries and whimpers from the injured.

Jim found that when morning came there was a bit more room in the boat. He was too exhausted to consider why. But during the night those who were the weakest had perished, and their bodies had been heaved overboard.

Suddenly he heard the drone of an aircraft approaching. Jim felt a mixture of hope and dread. Would this plane drop life rafts or bombs? Would the pilot radio a ship to come and help the survivors or would the plane make a turn and then swoop in low to destroy them?

Jim didn't know what to expect and so he simply watched in fear as the plane approached, descending from a pink morning sky.

The plane had an American insignia, and a signal lamp winked down at the castaways. Survivors decided the plane, having banked sharply just above them, meant no harm, and many started shouting and wildly waving pieces of clothing. The plane flew a couple of circles above the boat and then left, the hum of its engines fading.

Jim knew the pilots had seen them, and he allowed his spirits to rise, thinking that the men in the aircraft would send help. He thought a ship would arrive to rescue him in just a day or two. Doris, like Jim, was confident a ship would come, and she expected more planes to pass overhead, perhaps dropping water in containers. But hours went by, and no more aircraft were seen. Most survivors fell silent, each wondering if the planes really meant their nightmare would soon be over.

Some of the officers conducted an inventory of useful items in the boat and found precious little: a knife, oars, a bucket, bailing tins, a compass, some rope, and a container of lead putty that could be used to plug small leaks. Besides what scant clothing the survivors had on when they escaped the *Laconia*, there were only two blankets and a couple of small pieces of canvas that could be used for shelter from the sun and protection from the night's chill. The thing they needed most—water—was in a meager fifteen-gallon container. An adult needs approximately half a gallon of water a day to stay in good health: with sixty-eight people on board, the water in the container wouldn't last long. They were more than six hundred miles from the coast of Africa—which would take weeks to reach by drifting or even rowing. It was clear they would all die of dehydration long before reaching land if it didn't rain.

The food situation was no better than the water quantity. There were several tins of rock-hard biscuits, a bit of chocolate, some Horlick's malted milk tablets, and a few tins of pemmican.

Around midday the officers asked for attention. "We must set a course and get moving," one of them said. "It's pointless hanging around and hoping for rescue or a miracle. The German captain said land is north-north-east and six to seven hundred miles, so we'd better start rowing. Those who are physically able will have to take their turn at the oars."

No one debated with the officers. This was surprising, considering that the pilots in the plane had clearly seen them. Maybe a ship would be sent. But perhaps because of all the grief that the bomber had caused the day before, not a single survivor argued to keep the lifeboat as close to its current position as possible or to just drift.

Jim decided rowing was better than doing nothing. It would give him a sense of purpose. Jim moved toward the rowing station in the middle of the boat, glad for his first opportunity to sit down on one of the benches, or thwarts, next to the oars. He promptly picked up an oar and began the tedious process of stroking under a sun that was much too strong for his pale skin. An officer kept an eye on the compass and made sure their direction was true.

Over and over Jim dipped the oar, pulled back against the water, then lifted it from the sea to reposition and repeat the motion. Soon his mouth felt as dry as a desert.

A man sitting motionless caught Jim's attention. The man said, "I can't row. It's my hands." He held up his bloody, mangled hands. "I went over the side of the ship on a rope. Slid all the way down to the water."

Jim didn't know what to say, but he admired the man for not complaining or crying. The rope had taken the skin from the man's hands, and now they were useless stumps on the end of his arms, the fingers barely attached. There were no medical supplies on the lifeboat, so there was nothing Dr. Purslow could do. Jim feared the man's hands would soon become infected from the oily water left by the *Laconia*.

Others on the boat were also in bad shape, with deep cuts and torn skin. Jim's own injury, the gash on his calf from the barracuda bite, wasn't quite as bad as some of the wounds on fellow castaways, but it was susceptible to infection. If only he had kept his feet inside the boat when he first boarded he wouldn't have the throbbing ache from the wound.

While Jim rowed, others noticed the boat was leaking and started to bail water. Two sailors from the *Laconia* hunted for the source of the leak and eventually found it at the very bottom, where there was a gap between two old timbers. To reach the spot they removed three pieces of wood that covered an airtight tank (a safety feature to keep the boat afloat if it capsized). The resourceful men stripped some fibers from a rope and mixed them with a bit of lead putty to seal the crack. They put one of the boards back over the buoyancy tank and scrawled SOS on top with the white putty. They spread the other boards on the bottom of the boat so that Doris and Lady Grizel would have a dry area to sit.

Doris, a stout woman with a friendly, round face, was only wearing a damp petticoat. A considerate sailor gave her his thick, gray shirt. Other sailors gave Lady Grizel dry clothing and a blanket. The two women greatly appreciated this kindness. While Doris was in relatively good health, Lady Grizel was not. She was four months pregnant and had had some kidney issues even before the sinking. Doris comforted Lady Grizel as best she could, concerned about her friend's weakening condition. They talked of home and the things they would do back in England. Both women tried not to think of what might happen if a rescue ship didn't come soon.

SECOND CHANCE FOR SURVIVAL

TONY LARGE, LIFEBOAT #2

September 16–17

AFTER U-156 ABANDONED ITS RESCUE EFFORTS, LEAVING men and women in the water among the wreckage from the bombs, many people drowned. "Death was all around us," Tony Large recalled.

The young sailor with dark, wavy hair and a gap between his front teeth was too busy with his own survival to help anyone else. Just minutes after he climbed inside his righted lifeboat, desperate Italians swarmed the craft, tipping it over again.

Tired, angry, and frustrated, Tony repeatedly punched one Italian man in the head as they both hung on to the hull of the lifeboat. The man hardly resisted Tony's weak blows, which were an outlet for his roiling emotions.

Eventually the lifeboat was righted again, and Tony collapsed from both exhaustion and the mental strain of his seesaw feelings. First there had been the rush to escape *Laconia*, followed by the fear of being crammed into an unstable lifeboat. Then there was hope when the American plane first appeared. Next came terror during the bombing, and finally utter despair and disgust as he was left to an uncertain fate. Would he be rescued, or would death come slowly through periods of freezing nights and sweltering, thirsty days? After a while Tony felt numb as the damaged and overfilled lifeboat capsized again and again. Fewer people climbed back in each time. Then a shape appeared nearby.

It was another submarine, but its dark brown hull appeared to be different.

Instead of a German sub, this was the Italian *Cappellini*, sent by Dönitz to aid in the rescue of *Laconia* survivors. Like U-156, it was mostly concerned with the welfare of the Italian POWs but extended a hand to British refugees as well.

The submarine slowly glided closer, its long body sheltering several lifeboats from waves and wind. Instead of towing the boats as U-156 had done, Commander Marco Revedin encouraged the survivors to swim to the submarine. Tony was more than willing to leave the floundering lifeboat that was half filled with water for the relative security of the submarine's deck.

Tony, along with seventeen British soldiers and sailors, were hauled aboard the Italian sub. Some Italian POWs were already on board. Tony and most of the others huddled for warmth in the protective shadow of the *Cappellini*'s conning tower.

They were able to communicate basic information to Revedin, who peered at them from the top of the conning tower several feet above.

Laconia's dwindling number of Italian prisoners who managed to get aboard the *Cappellini* were soon taken inside while most of the British were left on the deck. Like Schacht on U-507, Revedin took a couple of British officers inside the submarine as prisoners of war.

The British refugees sheltering on the submarine's deck were warned that *Cappellini* would not hesitate to submerge if an enemy aircraft appeared. Revedin would not expose his crew to the hazardous risk that Hartenstein had experienced earlier that day. While Tony and his companions accepted the peril they were in, they preferred the safety of the submarine over that of their sinking lifeboat.

At dusk a crewman appeared with hot rice soup, bread, and cups of coffee, the most nourishing meal the men had consumed since dinnertime on the *Laconia* four days earlier.

During the night the submarine's engines started. The vessel began slowly moving through the ocean, waves lapping at the legs of the fearful British men clinging to the deck. There were no rails or lifelines to hold on to, so there was very little opportunity to rest.

In the morning *Cappellini* crewmen brought up the dead bodies of two Italian prisoners from the *Laconia* and dropped them into the ocean. Despite their relative safety, death was never far from Tony and his companions.

Two lifeboats were seen from the *Cappellini* the next day. One was passed at a distance. The other was nearby and contained another thirty Italians.

The French ships were expected that day but never appeared, leaving the *Cappellini* in a quandary. Staying near the scene of the *Laconia* sinking was dangerous, and feeding its survivors depleted the submarine's supplies.

Commander Revedin brought the second lifeboat close and had the Italians transferred to *Cappellini.* Then Tony and his nineteen British companions were instructed to get in the lifeboat, bringing the number of people in the boat to fifty-one. The prospect of imminent rescue, along with the boat's steel construction, raised their spirits somewhat. The Italian sub provided biscuits and eleven bottles of water before motoring away.

Tony tried to assess the probability of rescue. It had been five days since the *Laconia* was torpedoed and disappeared beneath the waves.

ALMOST 700 MILES TO AFRICA

TONY LARGE, LIFEBOAT #2

Approximately September 17–20

Tony Large expected help to come within hours. The submarine commander had said he would find a Vichy French ship that was nearby and escort it back to rescue them. Everyone was feeling optimistic that their suffering would soon be over. Little did they know that they would never see the Italian sub again and that no rescue ship was heading their way.

The lifeboat was twenty-eight feet long, and unlike most of the others from the *Laconia*, this one was made of steel. It was seaworthy and had a couple of benches, but there was no shelter from the sun.

The vessel lacked a rudder for steering and had only two oars, one of which was broken. The only other piece of equipment was an axe. With fifty-one men now on board, they could barely move. Food and water were in short supply. The boat held two one-gallon cans of water in addition to the eleven bottles left by the *Cappellini*. Tony estimated the total quantity of water at three or four gallons. (In normal times fifty-one adults would consume this amount in just a few hours.) Like Jim and Doris's vessel, Tony's lifeboat had some pieces of chocolate, malted milk tablets, biscuits, and pemmican.

The highest-ranking military man on the vessel was a Royal Air Force officer. He was put in charge of the food and water and made sure it was distributed equally. The officer did not give orders but instead made sure everyone had input on decisions. The direction they ultimately followed was based on a general consensus of the group.

As that first day dragged on without a ship arriving, many of the survivors realized that perhaps help wouldn't come for days, or maybe never. It was decided that food and water should be severely rationed and given out only in the evening. Each man was allowed just a tablespoon of water. How long they could live on such a meager amount was something they tried not to think about.

Worried that they might drift too far from possible rescue, they devised a sea anchor, which was used to slow the vessel's drift in the wind. The men tied together life jackets, adding some weight so they would sink, and secured it to a long line. They threw it overboard and let it drag far behind the lifeboat, slowing the boat down despite the breeze.

On September 20, when two and a half days had gone by without the arrival of a ship, the group decided that their only hope was to try to get to Africa. They surmised that the bulge of West Africa lay somewhere to their north, the same direction as the current was traveling and the direction of the gentle breezes.

Not wanting to rely solely on drifting, the men created a crude sailing rig. They used the one intact oar for the mast. With the axe, they fashioned a boom—the horizontal pole that holds the bottom of the sail—from a long piece of wood from one of the benches. Shirts and raincoat linings were fastened together and used as the sail. They used the broken oar as a rudder for steering.

They stowed the sea anchor aboard the vessel, and slowly the boat began sailing in a northerly direction. Three or four Allied planes, some near and some far, droned high in the sky, but none of them dipped their wings, the signal the survivors had hoped to see. After being bombed by an Allied plane, the castaways had little hope that a plane would initiate a rescue.

Tony tried to take his mind off his plight by watching the sea, examining the life in it. There were plenty of flying fish, which could glide for more than twenty feet over the surface of the water. A lone shark, about eight to ten feet in length, lazily followed the boat. When a whale appeared, Tony was fascinated, but also a bit fearful when it swam under them and reappeared on the other side. Had it decided to scratch its back on the boat's keel or bump the boat as if it were another whale, all fifty-one men would have surely ended up in the water.

By taking action to start sailing, albeit slowly at two miles per hour, the survivors felt their morale improve. But their thirst was so great that almost every waking moment was focused on the evening: That's when they would get their allotment of water. Their parched mouths could not generate enough saliva to force down the pemmican or biscuits, and it took considerable time to swallow a miniscule piece of chocolate.

There was almost no conversation. Mouths were too dry, and there was little to say. Tony learned about the men directly on either side of him, but beyond that range he had little contact with the others. When the shark swam off, a few men took a risk and swam briefly in the ocean. The seawater temporarily cooled them. During the swim a sea turtle popped up, and one of the swimmers made a grab for it, thinking he might be able to wrestle it aboard and they could eat it. The turtle, however, was much too strong and simply dove down and disappeared.

The swimmers did gather and eat some soft-shelled barnacles pulled from the submerged hull of the lifeboat. Tony thought they tasted fine. But the swimming sessions did not last long because the swimmers soon realized they barely had the strength to climb back into the boat. Their only other food during those first three days adrift—besides what little was stored in the boat and a couple of barnacles—was one small bird that landed on the vessel and was captured. Some men tried to eat tiny pieces of the bird, but the taste was so bad they spit it out.

Tony knew they would need additional food, but much more crucial was water. He looked to the sky for the possibility of a rain cloud, but only the blistering sun shone down on them.

Chapter 17

SALVATION, BUT NOT FOR EVERYONE

JOSEPHINE FRAME AND MOLLY DAVIDSON, VICHY FRENCH CRUISER *GLOIRE*

September 17–18

After spending a night aboard U-507, Josephine Frame was told by the U-boat commander that she would have to leave. Commander Schacht explained that women and children would have to go back to their lifeboats but that rescue was coming soon. Rested and refreshed by water and food, she didn't complain. Schacht smiled at her and said, "You didn't know you were underwater all night, did you?"

When Josephine reached the deck of the submarine, four lifeboats were clustered nearby. Her father helped her get back into the boat, which was being tossed by rough seas. He looked less hollow eyed than before, probably due to the stew the sub's cook dispensed. Fewer people were in the boat, giving everyone a small measure of space.

Soon the French cruiser *Gloire* appeared with its blue, white, and red flag flying, and the lifeboats rowed toward it.

When they were alongside the ship, survivors climbed up the scramble net (like a bunch of rope ladders strung together). French sailors helped them onto the deck. Some people were very weak; others' legs were unstable.

When the French warship picked up people from the lifeboats, there was one universal reaction: relief. Josephine remembers standing on an upper deck of *Gloire*, looking down at their empty lifeboat. As it bobbed in the waves, inching farther away from the ship, she was overcome by emotion. It was a mix of gratitude and pure exhaustion after so many days of worry. It felt good to be standing on a solid deck again, uncrowded, and with a hint of optimism.

The first order of business conducted by the *Gloire* officers was to separate the British men from the women. One officer recorded everyone's name and address. Women were given the officers' quarters while men were divided among other spaces like mess halls and galleries, where they were held under guard. None of the accommodations were luxurious, but none were so bad that anyone complained. Men stretched out anywhere they could, including under tables and on floors. It didn't matter, they were glad to be heading back to solid land.

The French crew, short on supplies for their own men, offered the *Laconia* survivors coffee laced with cognac and some bread.

The *Gloire* was a cruiser nearly as large as *Laconia* at 588 feet long, with a crew of more than five hundred. It was the largest and fastest of the three French ships rounding up *Laconia* survivors. The others were *Dumont d'Urville*, a much smaller sloop, and the small but fast sloop *Annamite*. Each sought opportunities to rendezvous with submarines carrying shipwreck survivors and to locate lifeboats that were quickly drifting from the intended meeting place, the spot where *Laconia* had sunk.

Dumont d'Urville was to pick up Italians from the

Cappellini, but in addition to the POWs, the sub had a surprise for them: survivors from the British merchant ship *Trevilley*, which was torpedoed by U-68 on September 12, the same day *Laconia* was hit by U-156.

Despite the seeming safety of the shipwreck refugees on the *Gloire*, more drama was unfolding. Back on Ascension Island, Captain Robert Richardson's pilots had seen the French ships, and British military in Freetown confirmed the ships had left the African mainland.

Richardson summoned his aircrew and began planning an attack.

On September 17, the day that the German submarines U-506 and U-507 were transferring people to the French ships, Richardson was in a B-24 that he flew over from Ascension. Staying clear of the big ship's antiaircraft guns, he claimed to observe the scene. He noted there was a German submarine floating close to the ship.

The next day, Richardson said he pulled together a squadron of attack aircraft, including a B-30 heavy bomber and some B-24s. He planned to attack *Gloire*. Witnessing the ship's cooperation with the U-boats automatically made the Vichy French an enemy, Richardson believed. He was sure they were only there to rescue Italians—and perhaps Germans who fled a sunken submarine.

As the bomber pilots were preparing their planes and checking their equipment for the mission to attack *Gloire*, Richardson informed US Navy intelligence about his plans. He was surprised when they told him to stand down.

Richardson's aircrews were forced to drop their plans to bomb *Gloire*.

Molly Davidson, who had spent the night on U-506 commanded by Würdemann, also made it aboard the *Gloire*, but it took her longer than Josephine. First Molly was picked up by the smaller *Annamite*, where she was surprised that the captain was friendly. He was somewhat apologetic, saying that he had to help the Germans because his family was in German-held territory in France.

After about a day and a half, the *Annamite* steamed to the larger *Gloire*. This occurred on September 19. Molly was exhausted and she certainly looked like a bedraggled castaway. She was now wearing a seaman's jacket and a bulky life jacket, both pulled over a tattered and dirty yellow dress. Her unkempt blond hair was matted to her scalp.

Molly was put aboard a life raft, which pulled up alongside the *Gloire*. She slowly climbed up the scramble net to the ship's deck.

She was greeted by shouts, "Molly! Molly! That's my daughter."

It had been several days since Molly Davidson and her mother lost track of each other. Each had held hope that they'd be reunited but stayed stoic, as if a crack in their certainty would bring a cascade of negative consequences.

The captain on the *Gloire* wasn't as friendly as the captain on the *Annamite*. While she felt relief to finally be aboard a ship and reunited with her mother, Molly had her concerns. She wondered what would happen to her. Although she was in the hands of Vichy French, the Germans were ultimately in control of her fate.

Gloire and the two other French ships continued to search a grid pattern of the ocean looking for more survivors. The lifeboats had drifted northwest from the site of the *Laconia* sinking at about fifteen miles per day. In the week after the torpedoing it was possible that some had traveled nincty miles in this direction. Some might have gone in a different direction entirely if they were sailing and steering purposely.

Nobody really knew how many lifeboats had been launched from *Laconia* during that chaotic night. Nor could anyone account for what happened to lifeboats after that, such as how many capsized from overfilling or how many were left after the American plane dropped its bombs. *Gloire*'s crew even found a handful of people still hanging on to life rafts days after the torpedoes struck.

FROM CASTAWAY TO POW

CLAUDE PARR

September 16–17

Claude Parr's lifeboat had traveled so far from the *Laconia* sinking that he never saw the Liberator drop its bombs. He and some other men were trying to catch fish. Even the smallest of fish might ease their hunger, and the moisture in the fish might help with hydration. The lack of a fishing hook did not thwart their efforts. Tying two shoelaces together they dangled them over the boat to attract the fish. When the fish bit the shoelace, men would dip their hands under the fish, and every now and then were successful in scooping a fish into the boat.

Claude had a hard time eating a couple of mouthfuls of raw fish. First he had trouble getting the portion down his dry throat, and then his stomach protested against the meal. Yet he still found the exercise of catching the fish helpful—it took his mind off the desperate situation in the cramped lifeboat.

Claude noticed a rapid deterioration in the men who were in their forties or older. They had become lethargic and needed to be coaxed to drink their tiny ration of water. As night approached, Claude realized these men had just hours to live. That was when fate intervened.

"I thought I saw lights," someone croaked as the lifeboat crested a wave. Most on board gave the man little notice. By this time people's thoughts were jumbled, and Claude would not have been surprised if survivors were starting to hallucinate.

Then when the boat crested the next wave, Claude and a few others saw the lights. They let out a raspy cheer and watched in nervous anticipation as a ship steamed on the horizon. Soon they realized the ship was moving away from them, and their hopes were cruelly dashed. Claude knew that the distance between the two vessels was too great for the sailors on the ship to see the lifeboat.

But one of the survivors snatched a flare from the small store of supplies. By removing the cap and rubbing the end of the flare against the cap he was able to ignite it and then waved it frantically. The castaways held their breath. This was their last chance. If the ship went by, the weaker survivors would surely start dying the next day.

Claude felt the seconds pass as if they were hours. One of the survivors stood and waved the flare above his head.

Was anyone on the ship's deck looking in their direction? Could a person on the ship even see such a tiny flare from hundreds of yards away? Those who had the strength to talk asked a question no one could answer, "Did they see us?"

They all watched the ship continue steaming ahead.

And then the ship seemed to slow down. The survivors held their breath. Yes, it was turning toward them! A raspy cheer erupted from Claude and several others.

A spotlight on the ship swept the ocean. The

vessel kept coming in the direction of the castaways. Then the spotlight settled on the lifeboat. Claude took to the oars, and he and a few other men who still had a bit of strength started rowing toward the ship.

When the lifeboat was alongside the ship, a ladder was lowered. They really were being rescued. This was no mirage.

Those who were strong enough climbed the ladder—and were greeted by two men with bayonets on their rifles. The ship was the *Gloire*, controlled by the Vichy French. This meant that Claude and the other survivors were now prisoners and faced an uncertain future. But anything was better than being trapped in a lifeboat with no water on the endless sea.

Some people in the lifeboat were too feeble to move, and sailors from the ship carried them aboard. They were given water, then put in a holding area and placed under guard and spent the rest of the night packed tightly together lying on a steel floor. The lone woman was allowed the comfort of a cabin room.

While not the welcome Claude had hoped for, he soon realized just how lucky they were that they had been found. Earlier, the *Gloire* had steamed to the *Laconia* sinking site and rescued many survivors such as Molly and Josephine. Then after a brief search without finding any other castaways alive, the ship headed for Dakar. It was sheer luck that the vessel passed near enough to Claude's lifeboat to see the flare. Claude also didn't realize that a German U-boat commander had alerted the Vichy French ships to come rescue the *Laconia* survivors.

Claude wasn't worried about being a prisoner of war after what he endured on the lifeboat, and he thought he might soon be free. Little did he know that this part of his ordeal was going to have its own set of challenges and freedom was uncertain.

DANGEROUS BEGINNINGS OF DEHYDRATION

JIM MCLOUGHLIN AND DORIS HAWKINS, LIFEBOAT #1

Approximately September 17–20

Doris Hawkins was strong in body and mind, and determined to live despite the long odds. She had shown her grit in the ocean right after escaping the *Laconia* when drowning men had clawed at her and she had fought them off. And both she and Lady Grizel had the benefit of receiving some food and water while on the U-boat—an opportunity not all castaways had.

The food and water allotment on this second day aboard the lifeboat was pathetically small. In the morning everyone received two malted milk tablets and a piece of chocolate. Water was strictly limited to a meager tablespoon served in a small biscuit tin. Their mouths were so dry that the water was instantly absorbed in their cheeks and tongues before they had a chance to swallow. Pieces of the rock-hard biscuit with a touch of pemmican spread were passed around. Again the survivors had trouble swallowing even the smallest portions of the dry biscuit. Jim's technique of getting sustenance from the biscuit was to put a tiny piece in his mouth and simply wait for it to become soft. Then he struggled to swallow it, with parts of the biscuit getting stuck in his dry throat.

These castaways were in the mild first stage of dehydration, where they had lost approximately 5 percent of their body's fluids. Besides the incredible thirst and dry mouth, other symptoms can include headache and rapid breathing. The moderate next stage, with 10 percent loss of body fluid, brings about a loss of mental performance, irritability, and reduced urinary output. A person reaches the extreme stage when more than 10 percent of bodily fluids are lost.

That's when people have difficulty concentrating and comprehending, in addition to rapid breathing, severe headaches, and possible hallucinations. Eventually blood pressure falls and the person collapses. Death will quickly follow without a drink of water.

In addition to dehydration, the searing sun was wreaking havoc on the castaways. Should their body temperature rise above 106 degrees, they would experience heat stroke, bringing death sooner.

The castaways had suffered under the sun's burning rays all day, but at night the temperature plunged into the lower 60s, and they were chilled to the bone. Doris and Lady Grizel huddled together under the blanket for warmth but still shivered throughout the night. Gusts of cold wind sucked their body heat away, and every now and again they were soaked by a breaking wave. Their cold limbs ached, and they did their best to stretch in the cramped confines of the vessel.

Jim, whose barracuda-bitten leg throbbed more as the temperature dropped, decided to keep rowing. He had no illusion that they would reach land, but wanted to do his part moving the vessel closer to Africa, where perhaps there would be shipping traffic.

The effort of rowing helped warm Jim a bit, but exhaustion soon overtook the young man, and his chin dropped to his chest. He rowed as if in a trance, the hypnotic motion freeing his mind to roam. At one point during the night he heard a disturbance followed by a splash. He was too tired to think what caused the commotion, but later learned a person had been pushed overboard. Jim wasn't sure if the victim was dead or if the others decided to make more room for themselves by tossing one of the weakest survivors into the sea. The realization that this was a possibility frightened him to the core.

When dawn broke, there was still no sign of a rescue ship. Some of the men rigged a piece of canvas between two oars to act as a sail, and others continued to row. Most survivors had lost hope that a ship would come. They had not seen other lifeboats since the plane dropped the bombs, nor had they any idea where a rendezvous with a ship would occur if one did come. And so the officers, and most of the survivors, continued to believe they had a better chance of being found if they moved closer to land.

It was now approximately September 19, and the day was little different from the previous one: scorching sun and the monotony of an endless sea. Jim curled up in the forward section of the boat and tried to get what little sleep he could. His tongue was swollen from lack of moisture, and his arms ached from rowing.

Doris and Lady Grizel also moved closer to the front of the boat, where a bit of periodic shade could be found in the shadow of the makeshift sail. The three castaways talked a bit, and Jim was impressed by Doris's attempt at good cheer and even a bit of humor. She addressed him as McLoughlin rather than Jim, and Jim in turn began to call her Freckles because the strong sun had brought out freckles all over Doris's burnt skin. Doris and Jim looked after each other, offering comforting words when they spoke, and both did their best to ease the suffering of Lady Grizel, who was clearly failing.

That evening Jim went back to rowing and sometime during the night heard a diesel engine. He sat erect and fully alert, trying to determine where the sound was coming from. This could be the help they so desperately needed.

Suddenly a submarine pushed out of the darkness, and a group of submarine sailors shouted, "*Italiano? Italiano?*"

The sub was the Italian *Cappellini*, and the men on board wanted to know whether anyone in the lifeboat was from their country.

When the men on the lifeboat hollered back "No, no Italians here," the sub moved off and was never seen again.

Jim felt numb, confused, and utterly depressed. The appearance of the sub was brief, and he tried not to think too much about it as he went back to rowing. Subs and planes...but no rescue ship. Jim had a hard time reconciling that people knew the *Laconia* survivors were adrift but no one was helping them. He was slowly coming to accept that there would be no rescue. He knew that if he was to have any chance of survival, he must simply hang on for as long as he could and hope that closer to land a ship would spot them.

The next day Doris did her best to keep Jim's spirits up. They each described their homes and spoke confidently about their willpower to endure until salvation came.

Doris broke her boredom—and her nonstop thoughts of drinking a cool glass of water—by gazing over the side of the boat and looking at the colorful fish. Occasionally the fin of a shark would make her shudder, but fear was later replaced by awe when whales approached the vessel. She marveled at how they noisily spouted jets of water high into the air.

When the whales left, Doris returned to yearning for the water ration in the evening. "My worst torture was thirst," she recalled. "I could easily bear the lack of food. When each water ration was passed around everyone [looked at] it with longing as it went from hand to hand."

When Doris got her ration, she didn't drink it down but instead stretched the wonderful sensation out as long as she could. She'd take a tiny sip, then swirl it around her gums until it was absorbed, and then do the same with the next. The relief that the tablespoon of water provided lasted no more than a couple of minutes.

Doris and Jim knew they wouldn't last much longer with so little water, but both had a steely resolve to fight on.

Chapter 20

AN AXE-SWINGING MADMAN

TONY LARGE, LIFEBOAT #2

Approximately September 21–23

LATER IN TONY'S FIRST WEEK ADRIFT, ONE MAN named Butch devised a way to capture some fish. Butch was a heavily muscled man who Tony thought was arrogant but grudgingly acknowledged was the best fisherman.

Butch had found a large nail in the boat and was able to bend it with the axe into a hook. He scraped the nail with the axe to make it shine. Then he tied the hook to a three-foot length of thin line, probably from clothing or a strand from a larger boat line, and lowered it down to a school of silver fish that swam under the vessel. The fish couldn't resist biting the shiny nail. Although most squirmed their way off the makeshift hook, several were hauled aboard.

Fresh water, rather than food, was what the castaways needed most. Some became so desperate that they took sips of seawater. While it may have provided instant relief, drinking seawater will soon kill a person. Instead of adding moisture to a needy body, the salt content does the opposite. Seawater has four times the sodium that our bodily fluids have, and in an attempt to dilute the salt water coming in, our cells excrete some of their own moisture. The kidneys are activated by the excessive amount of salt, and that causes more frequent urination, expelling both the seawater and some of the body's own less salty fluids from cells. The result is that seawater dehydrates the person who consumes it. Usually, the first sign of this rapid dehydration comes in the form of hallucinations.

Tony did not know all the physiological harm drinking seawater could cause, but he instinctively understood it would lead to problems if ingested.

Butch, however, thought the opposite. He drank a little seawater in both the morning and the evening. Butch then supplemented the seawater by drinking his own urine. This too has harmful side effects on the body. When a person is healthy and hydrated, about 95 percent of urine is water, but the other 5 percent is waste products including sodium. A hydrated person can drink a small amount with no ill effects. But swallowing more than a small amount of urine is disastrous to the body's organs, especially the kidneys. Instead of ridding the body of toxins, drinking urine puts those same toxins right back into the body. And when a person is dehydrated the urine is darker and more concentrated with waste, making it even more dangerous.

Butch did not immediately get sick from his sips of seawater and urine, so some of the fellow castaways started to do the same. Tony, however did not, and instead told himself that somehow he would survive, while at the same time praying for rain.

The grim hand of death soon took hold of the lifeboat. The ones who died first were the survivors following Butch's lead of drinking seawater and urine.

Tony could usually tell who was going to expire because "those men lost their capacity to relate to others, lost interest in everything around them including their evening sip of [fresh] water, a bad, bad sign, and they died almost every one of them at night."

Many of those who drank seawater started acting strangely, talking but not making sense, seeing things that weren't there. Some of the hallucinations were pleasant, some terrifying. Their bodies were experiencing chemical reactions as their cells unsuccessfully tried to expel microscopic amounts of moisture to offset the shock of so much salt in their systems. The cells included brain cells, and this last-ditch effort of the body to put more moisture into their bloodstream caused delirium. Tony looked on in horror as each man who drank the deadly seawater responded in different ways. Their minds were no longer within their control.

Butch survived two days after drinking the lethal combination of seawater and urine. The mixture caught up with him, and he expired one night. He died quietly and did not become violent or try to move about the boat. Tony and several other men pushed and pulled Butch's body to the side of the vessel and dropped him into the sea.

Perhaps the scariest moments aboard the lifeboat occurred when dehydration caused delirium. A man suddenly grabbed the axe and began swinging it at the other men, and then at the bottom of the boat. If the man wasn't stopped, those who were still fighting to live might become victims of this man's derangement.

Because the vessel was made of steel, the man's hacking with the axe did not put a hole in the hull. Tony tried to calmly reason with him, but the man swung the axe at Tony's head, narrowly missing him. Some other men jumped on the back of the delirious man and subdued him.

The lifeboat became still, and the castaways did their best to get through the day. They were in such a weak state that most just sat in a stupor with nowhere to hide from the searing sun. Tony closed his eyes and tried to preserve what little energy he had left.

Suddenly, the man got hold of the axe again and started swinging it at nearby survivors. Other men tackled him, took the axe away, and determined the man was a mortal threat to all of them. Worried that he would spring back up and start punching people or try to tip the boat over, the survivors decided their only choice was to throw him overboard.

Tony felt terrible about this decision but agreed there was no other viable option. The man would likely have died anyway from drinking seawater. Tony and the others had to think of the larger picture: the safety of the group.

The delirious man had lost all ability to control his actions and he was a threat to the rest of the group, which now numbered about thirty out of the original fifty-one.

The older leaders, including the Royal Air Force officer, started succumbing near the end of the first week in the lifeboat. They mostly perished from dehydration.

Tony became responsible for handing out the drinking water. This responsibility, plus his unshakable belief that somehow he would see his family again, helped him stay sane. He had frequent dreams, many of which were actually pleasant. He dreamed about food and his home quite often, but he also had a vivid dream of his father walking across the water to the lifeboat. Another time he dreamed of a destroyer arriving to rescue the castaways and how he later visited a cool, babbling brook. Dreaming, however, did not solve the water shortage, and Tony knew he and the remaining survivors could not hold on much longer.

STEELY TENACITY

JIM MCLOUGHLIN AND DORIS HAWKINS, LIFEBOAT #1

Approximately September 22–26

While Claude, Molly, and Josephine were being transported to land on the *Gloire*, Jim and Doris were suffering through their sixth day adrift since the Liberator bombed U-156.

Rowing was nearly impossible for Jim because of his lack of strength and the chafing of his raw hands by the oars. One of the sailors made a small sail out of a piece of canvas and attached it to an oar that he kept upright with pieces of rope. It wasn't much, but the boat did respond, and those still alert were thankful for the feeling they were moving through the water rather than adrift.

To help alleviate the torment from the blistering sun, some of the men secured two of the oars across the middle of the boat from side to side, or gunwale to gunwale. Then they fixed two blankets over the oars and added pieces of clothing to make a shaded spot at the bottom of the vessel. They took turns crawling into the shelter to escape the sun. But when night came those who had contributed the articles of clothing took them back to ward off the cold.

One night, Jim lay on the bottom of the boat, his arms clasped around his chest seeking to retain some of the warmth his body tried to generate. His arms, legs, and back were stiff from the cold, and his ragged clothing was wet from the seawater that sloshed around. In his torpid state the minutes passed agonizingly slowly. He watched the starless black sky begin to show the first hint of dawn, turning a slate gray hue. As the minutes crawled by, more of dawn's light brightened the gloom above him.

Jim always looked forward to first light because it was often accompanied by a fine mist. He tilted his head back and opened his parched mouth. The moisture in the air often produced a drop or two of rain. While the boat rocked, he closed his eyes, kept his mouth open, and hoped this would be the day a downpour would come. It did not.

Doris thought the sight of the men with their heads thrown back and dry brown tongues hanging out of open mouths was one of the saddest scenes she had ever witnessed.

While that little bit of moisture made dawn something to look forward to, the light would also reveal who had died during the night. To be sure they were dead, Dr. Purslow searched for a pulse. Then, with sadness and a frustration born of helplessness, the doctor would shake his head and say, "Looks like he's gone." The bodies were stripped of whatever rags of clothing clung to them, then dragged to the gunwale and pushed overboard.

The doctor himself could barely move, so Doris assisted in this grim process, going from body to body and looking for signs of life. If she wasn't sure the person was dead, she vigorously rubbed their faces and hands, hoping to get the blood flowing. Every now and then her efforts yielded results, and people who appeared dead would moan or lift a hand. Doris would offer comfort, but in most cases they would only last another day.

Jim's determination to live was shaken by the non-stop moaning from all who suffered. He wondered if it was worth it to keep enduring, which meant continued pain. If he simply gave up, death would come sooner, and the suffering would end. Watching dead bodies being slipped over the side of the lifeboat on a daily basis also weakened his resolve. Yet Jim watched Doris handling each day with a steely tenacity. She was not only persisting, she was comforting others, and that—along with thinking of his family—gave Jim the inspiration to fight on.

Doris was so strong-willed that she still appreciated the beauty of the ocean and the sky above. She especially found the sunsets pleasing, when the sky "was a blaze of glory, reflected in the sea, and the afterglow of colors which spread and lasted till the blue shadows of night stretched across and took their place."

If it was a clear night, Doris set her gaze on the

moon and the twinkling stars that she thought more brilliant than those in the English sky. She felt the stars were encouraging her to stay strong and endure through the night. In the morning she greeted the day with new hope: *Surely today will be the day of rescue*, she thought.

Doris's courage, however, was under constant attack by the combination of her unbearable thirst and the blistering sun. By midmorning the heat was intense and the sun rays burned strong. She did her best to protect both herself and Lady Grizel with rags of disintegrating clothing. Despite the heat, the survivors' bodies were so dry they did not perspire.

As mornings inched into afternoons, Doris tried to sleep but instead found herself light-headed and could only doze intermittently. She dreamed of ice cream, mangoes, giant glasses of pineapple juice, and simple cups of tea. "Over and over again, teasing and tormenting, like a cinematography show, the scenes passed and re-passed," she recalled. Each time she awoke from the fitful dozing she promised herself she would never waste water, never let a dripping tap continue to run. To Doris, fresh water had become the most precious thing on earth.

As Doris and Jim entered their second week adrift in the lifeboat, they noticed a rapid deterioration in both Lady Grizel and Dr. Purslow. Lady Grizel, who had talked with Doris and even kept her sense of humor, laughing softly at Doris's jokes or something amusing said by the men, was now mostly quiet. Despite her suffering she never complained and always thanked Doris for whatever comfort the nurse could provide.

Then, on September 25, Lady Grizel somehow knew she would not survive the day. She thanked Doris for all she had done, adding, "We've had lots of fun." Then she gave Doris her home address, so her family could be told exactly what happened to her.

Doris held the ill woman in her arms throughout the night, trying her best to keep her warm. Lady Grizel slept soundly, and at sunrise she simply stopped breathing, dying peacefully in Doris's arms.

Despite his own weakness Dr. Purslow crawled across the boat to Doris, Jim, and the lifeless Lady Grizel. He led the living in a prayer. Doris suggested they try to sing the hymn "Abide with Me."

Abide with me; fast falls the eventide;
The darkness deepens; Lord with me abide.
When other helpers fail and comforts flee,
Help of the helpless, O abide with me.

Swift to its close ebbs out life's little day;
Earth's joys grow dim; its glories pass away;
Change and decay in all around I see;
O Thou who changest not, abide with me.

Doris described their singing as "pathetic." With such parched mouths it's a wonder they even tried, but despite their wretched state they wanted to show both their faith and their respect for the woman who died so far from home.

Then they bade Lady Grizel a final goodbye and lowered her into the ocean.

Doris was heartbroken, and feeling alone. She was now the only woman on the lifeboat. But she rallied and repeated Lady Grizel's address to herself. She wanted to live so that she could tell Lady Grizel's loved ones about her struggles and how brave she was before her death. This became a mission of sorts for Doris—to inform family members of those who died about what had happened on the lifeboat. Before anyone was lowered into the ocean, Doris removed a personal possession such as a ring or a necklace to give to the families.

Although Doris didn't know it, her decision to bear witness and someday answer the questions of family members of the deceased gave her a sense of purpose that is a common trait among the toughest survivors. They don't give up because they want to complete their duty. Instead of just focusing on themselves, they have a higher calling, an objective to live for. Doris was more determined than ever to fight on. Her goal was to tell the world the sequence of events that befell those on the ill-fated *Laconia*.

Meanwhile, the number of living were decreasing daily on the lifeboat.

One of Doris's biggest frustrations was the same as Dr. Purslow's: the lack of any medical supplies. As a nurse, Doris could have done so much more to help those who were suffering the most if only she had drugs for infection or pain, and dressings for wounds. She and the doctor did the best they could for those afflicted by infected sores. They would open the infected spot with a penknife, then try and cleanse the area with salt water. Unfortunately, without clean bandages they could not cover the wound properly. They were careful to always wash the penknife in salt water as they explained to the patients the importance of not infecting each other.

Doris had the utmost respect for the young doctor. She realized he barely had any strength of his own, yet he continued to move around the boat doing his best to comfort the sick.

Jim and Doris watched Dr. Purslow's movements become slower and slower. They knew they needed some kind of lucky break—rain or a passing ship—for the doctor to stay alive.

A HARSH PENALTY

TONY LARGE, LIFEBOAT #2

Approximately September 24–30

AROUND THE EIGHTH OR NINTH DAY ADRIFT SINCE the bombing of U-156, eight men died in Tony's lifeboat within twenty-four hours. Now just twenty-two men were left from the original fifty-one.

With so many gone, the remaining survivors had enough room to stretch out and lie down. And with fewer men in the boat the fresh water supply didn't shrink as rapidly.

One night, near the end of September, Tony was awakened by shouts. He sat up in the dim light of the rising moon and looked where a survivor was pointing. A freighter was steaming perpendicular to the lifeboat, a mere three hundred to four hundred yards away!

The survivors shouted and blew their lone whistle. The freighter did not slow down. Someone picked up the axe and pounded it against the steel hull of the lifeboat, sending loud bangs reverberating into the night. Surely a lookout on the ship would hear the blows.

Still the ship kept moving. Survivors were screaming and shouting, but no one on the ship heard their cries, and the vessel disappeared into the darkness.

To have salvation so close and have nothing come of it was a crushing blow. One minute survivors were filled with fresh hope and the next they sank into despair. The incident broke the spirit of several men, and they were dead within a day. Others soon succumbed to the deadly practice of drinking seawater, and they too perished.

Tony was overcome by misery and dejection, but his inner strength would not allow him to give up. He vowed to fight on until his last breath.

The passing ship not only crushed the resolve of some men to live, it made one survivor do something that was unpardonable. A young soldier with an angular face was accused of sneaking a drink from the lone water canister. The soldier vigorously denied the charges of this ultimate betrayal. Tony had not seen the alleged incident, but he and the others warned the soldier that if he or any survivor was found stealing—or even meddling with the water can—the penalty would be severe. They would be tossed overboard.

Despite the warning, the next day the same young man was caught in the act. He was using a piece of rubber tubing: one end was in the water can and the other in his mouth. This time the soldier did not deny it. He knew his fate. He said he was sorry, took a big drink of seawater, and administered the penalty to himself by stepping over the side of the boat and swimming away.

The remaining survivors watched him go. No one said a word.

Every hour, every death, and every event that would be impossible to imagine in the civilized world was wearing Tony down. He did not think it could get worse. But it did.

Tony had formed a friendship with a Canadian air force officer whom he called Canada. He was a gentle and considerate soul, and prior to their tongues becoming too swollen and dry to talk, the two men had commiserated together and had gotten to know each other. Or so Tony thought.

Just a day or two after the close encounter with the ship, one of the survivors shouted, "Look, Canada!"

Tony glanced up and saw Canada calmly slip over the side of the boat and paddle away, never looking back, never saying a word.

For the first time in this nightmare Tony sobbed uncontrollably. He could do nothing to save his friend.

CREEPING MADNESS

JIM MCLOUGHLIN AND DORIS HAWKINS, LIFEBOAT #1

Approximately September 26–October 2

It almost seemed inevitable that some castaways on Jim and Doris's lifeboat would resort to drinking seawater, as they had on Tony's vessel. The thirst tormented them so much that it overruled sound decision-making. Despite warnings from Jim, Doris, and Dr. Purslow, a few of the survivors began this desperate act. Within hours they were talking gibberish or rambling nonsense about things only they could see.

Listening to these men put Doris in a dark place, and she tried to shut out the noise, afraid it would cause her to lose her ability to reason. She was suffering more than ever and forcing herself to eat her one mouthful of food per day. It took her an hour just to swallow a tiny bit of pemmican.

One of the men, Zdzislaw Uher, was able to eat a biscuit every day by dipping it in seawater to soften it, and suffered no harm from the practice. Doris did not want to take such a risk, but she was thankful when this same man had enough strength during the heat of the day to dip a canister into the ocean and pour the water over Doris's head for a bit of relief.

Jim knew that each day the number of people in the lifeboat diminished because of deaths. But now he wondered if some of the scuffling he heard during the night were the noises of the strong throwing one of the weak overboard so that the drinking water would last longer. He wasn't sure, but he tried to project strength—he did not want to look like one of the weak.

Jim's hunch was correct. Another survivor on his boat, Harold Gibson, later explained that the healthier men knew who was going to die next. He said he could tell who was going to die by their eyes. "Eyes tell you a lot. When they look at you with sad eyes they know they are dying. In fact some were wishing to die."

Gibson explained that in an effort to conserve drinking water some of the men decided to throw the weakest overboard while they were still alive. "We knew in our hearts they were going to be dead the next day so we just ditched them over the side and saved the water for those that were strong enough."

Was this act murder? Was it justified by the horrific conditions? Was Gibson trying to excuse his actions by saying "some were wishing to die"? Those questions are simply too difficult to answer. But Jim's determination to look strong was well-founded. He would not be sacrificed to the ocean so others could have more drinking water.

One night Jim lay awake in the bow, looking back toward the stern and saw the man who was controlling the tiller suddenly stand up and start singing.

"Show me the way to go home!" the man sang. "I'm tired and I want to go to bed."

Jim's eyes widened, terrified of what the man might do next. Like the words in the song it was likely the man did in fact take a drink, not of alcohol, but seawater. Another possibility was that he broke the lifeboat's compass, which was later found in pieces. Inside the compass was a tiny amount of alcohol that he might have drunk. Perhaps he drank both the alcohol and seawater. Whatever the reason, his thoughts were a jumbled mess.

The man sang another line or two and then, without any notice, jumped overboard.

Jim was shaken to the core that delirium was creeping through the boat. He could hear the man in the water still singing at the top of his lungs as he drifted away from the boat.

Jim started to fear each night. Adding to the gloom and eerie feeling was the phosphorescence—the glowing plankton—that twinkled in the wake of the slow-moving vessel. Jim felt like he was no longer on earth but in the spirit world, and he worried he was losing his own mind. He stayed at the bow of the vessel and rarely slept.

With the compass broken, the survivors had to navigate by the sun during the day and the stars at night. This was not as precise as using the compass, and some questioned if the navigation was getting them closer to shore. Like in Tony's lifeboat, a couple of men didn't wait for death to take them but simply crawled to the side of the vessel as they gave up hope altogether.

Both Jim and Doris fought to keep a grip on their emotions. The days were all blending together, and they no longer kept track of how long they had been adrift.

About two weeks into their terrible odyssey there was reason for hope. While staring out at the ocean, trying yet again to appreciate its ever-changing hues of greens, blues, and grays, Doris saw something on the horizon. Her eyes were dry and stinging from the lack of moisture and the glare of the sun, but she squinted, and on the crest of a small wave she saw the object again.

"Ship!" she croaked.

People who had the strength to sit up also saw the vessel. They shouted and waved, and one man even produced a whistle that he blew as loud as he could.

But the ship, a three-funnel vessel, was approximately four miles away. This was the opportunity they had all been waiting for, and they had to get the attention of the sailors on the ship. Using a cigarette lighter, which miraculously still functioned, they set fire to a life jacket, placed it in a bucket and held it aloft. Black smoke wafted into the air.

Doris prayed. *Surely the ship is turning*, she thought. Craning forward, she watched hopefully. *No, not yet.*

One of the men in the bow exclaimed, "She is nearer!"

Jim, shielding his eyes from the sun, thought it did appear the ship was getting nearer.

"That's the *Britannic*," Jim said, eyes fixed on the horizon. "She was in Cape Town when *Laconia* called in there. I remember her shape. A liner. A Cunard White Star ship."

Doris, Jim, and many of the others were now convinced rescue was imminent. Some talked of the food and the rum they would soon consume aboard the ship.

They waited. And waited. The ship kept moving at a steady pace. The man in the bow was wrong: the ship was not coming closer, nor had its lookout seen the lifeboat from such a distance.

Doris slumped back on the deck, feeling overwhelming despair.

One of the sailors muttered, "She didn't bloody well stop."

Jim responded that the men on the ship never saw the lifeboat. "We're a tiny boat low down in the water. It would've been a miracle if she'd seen us."

Having potential rescue so close and not come to fruition absolutely devastated the morale on the lifeboat. For some, this was a turning point, the time when they lost their will to live. It seemed that fate had conspired against them and that they were doomed to suffer alone on the endless sea. Once hope was gone, it was hard to carry on the fight.

One of the older officers tried to improve the group's spirits, saying, "We've had a big disappointment today, but there's always tomorrow. The fact that we have seen a ship means we are near a shipping route, and perhaps our luck will turn now."

But when another day went by with no ship in sight, more people lost hope and passed away.

Doris and Jim rallied from their despair and renewed their belief that somehow they would be saved. Doris and a couple of men led the group in prayer at night. They would need a miracle, fate, or incredible good luck to survive.

LOCATION OF *LACONIA* ATTACK

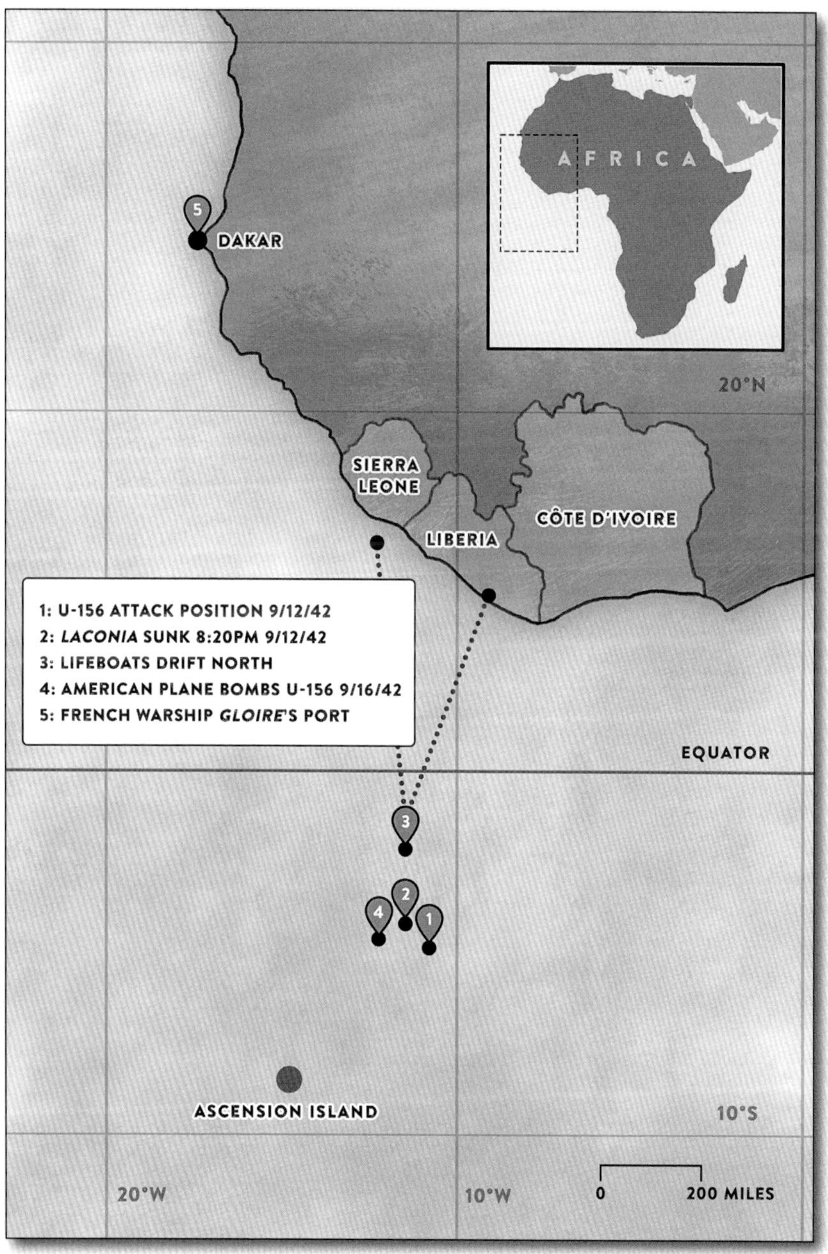

Art by Keith Robinson

(Above) Capt. Robert C. Richardson III seated in his P-47 Thunderbolt. He was the American army air force officer at Ascension Island who ordered the B-24 Liberator to bomb German submarine U-156 when it was covered in a Red Cross flag and sheltering survivors of the *Laconia* sinking.

Photo courtesy of Richardson family

(Left) Able Seaman Tony Large, a Durban, South Africa, native and member of the Royal Navy. He was shipwrecked by torpedoes twice in 1942.

Photo reproduction by James West, image courtesy of Large family

A passenger's boarding pass for *Laconia* that was used to record the deaths of people in the lifeboat with Tony Large as it drifted toward Africa.

British National Archives/ Photo by Alison O'Leary

(Left) Werner Hartenstein, commander of German submarine U-156, gave the order to torpedo the *Laconia*, then gave the order to rescue its shipwrecked passengers.

Photo courtesy of Deutsches U-Boot Museum

(Right) Harro Schacht, commander of German submarine U-507, tried to help *Laconia* shipwreck refugees to find family members among the lifeboats.

Photo courtesy of Deutsches U-Boot Museum

(Above) Laconia, an intercontinental ocean liner built for luxury, was taken over by the British government for military transportation in 1939. The black plume of smoke from its stack was seen by lookouts on U-156, which followed the ship for a day before firing torpedoes. In this photo the double rows of lifeboats are visible on the highest of the ship's seven decks.

Courtesy of British National Maritime Museum, Liverpool

(Left) Erich Würdemann, commander of German submarine U-506, rushed to assist with the shipwreck refugees, even submerging his vessel with more than 150 aboard.

Photo courtesy of Deutsches U-Boot Museum

The crew of German submarine U-156 standing on the deck and raised conning tower. British shipwreck refugees from the *Laconia* reported that the submarine had a "Bonzo dog" painted on it.

Photo courtesy of Deutsches U-Boot Museum

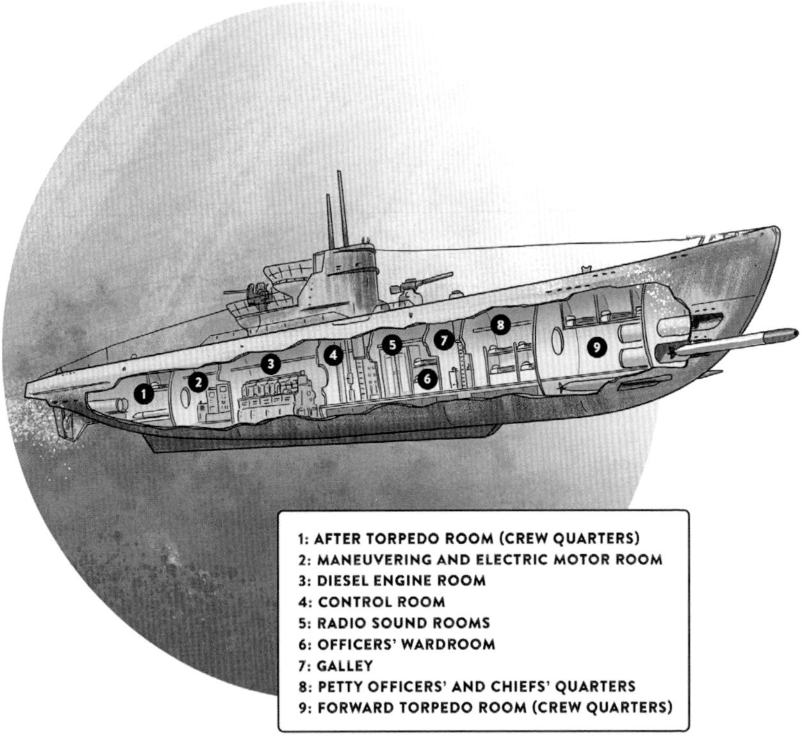

1: AFTER TORPEDO ROOM (CREW QUARTERS)
2: MANEUVERING AND ELECTRIC MOTOR ROOM
3: DIESEL ENGINE ROOM
4: CONTROL ROOM
5: RADIO SOUND ROOMS
6: OFFICERS' WARDROOM
7: GALLEY
8: PETTY OFFICERS' AND CHIEFS' QUARTERS
9: FORWARD TORPEDO ROOM (CREW QUARTERS)

Italian prisoners of war crowded on the deck of German submarine U-506 after the sinking of the *Laconia*, where they had been held in squalid conditions.
Photo courtesy of Deutsches U-Boot Museum

During the rescue mission of German submarines U-156, U-506, and U-507, crowded lifeboats with British sailors, soldiers, and civilian women and children were repaired and restocked with food and water. In this photo sailors from U-506 help *Laconia* passengers.
Photo courtesy of Deutsches U-Boot Museum

(Left) German type IX-C submarines were 250 feet long, 22 feet wide, were powered by both diesel and electric engines, and carried a crew of about fifty-two men for voyages that lasted up to four months.

Art by Keith Robinson

Laconia lifeboats were about 30 feet long, not designed for the panicked crowds of 80 or more people who jammed into them when the ship was sunk by a torpedo from German submarine U-156. In this photo a packed lifeboat is pulled next to submarine U-506 to aid Italian prisoners and provide food and water.

Photo courtesy of Deutsches U-Boot Museum

British women and children were well treated when they were brought inside German submarines after the *Laconia* was sunk. They would later spend weeks in prison camps in Africa. In this photo Molly Davidson is seated at far right.

Photo courtesy of Deutsches U-Boot Museum

German submarines were cautious about being close together when transferring refugees from the *Laconia* shipwreck. Here a raft is used to move people from one submarine to another so that each had about the same number of people aboard.

Photo courtesy of Deutsches U-Boot Museum

Many of the Italian prisoners from the *Laconia* were barely clothed when they were rescued by German submarines. The German crewmen provided clothing from their own lockers and also shared their food and skin cream, even showing family photos to the British women who sheltered in the submarines.

Photo courtesy of Deutsches U-Boot Museum

Molly Davidson was on her way home from the war-torn island of Malta in the Mediterranean Ocean when she and her mother boarded the *Laconia*. After dressing a man's wounds in a lifeboat and spending time aboard U-506, she lived at a prisoner-of-war camp in Morocco.

Photo courtesy of Lewes Family

Josephine Frame was planning to play a game with her brother Alex when the torpedoes hit the *Laconia*. The fourteen-year-old was fleeing the Japanese invasion of Singapore with her family when they boarded the ship.

Photo courtesy of Josephine Frame Pratchett

AND ONLY FOUR WERE LEFT

TONY LARGE, LIFEBOAT #2

Approximately October 3–9

About the first of October the number of survivors in Tony's lifeboat had dwindled to nine. Of the nine, four were still functioning and thinking relatively clearly. The other five barely moved or spoke.

Tony got to know one of the survivors quite well, Leading Seaman Harry Vines, who was a gunner on the *Laconia*. Although they could barely croak out a few words to each other, it was comforting to both of them to form a connection with someone whose mental state was intact. After losing his friend Canada, it was important to Tony to have someone else in the boat that he trusted and felt close to.

Keeping track of time was getting near impossible for Tony. Every day had been almost the same: misery, death, disappointment, and thirst. He guessed it was the first week of October when another bitter blow registered in Tony's weary mind. Because Tony was in charge of distributing the water, he knew exactly how much was left in the canister. There was only a day of rations left.

To keep the remaining survivors from giving up all hope, Tony told them he thought there were several days of water in reserve. The men may not have believed his deception. By now everyone, even Tony, had taken small sips of seawater. If they continued to do that, death might be violent. On the other hand, the sips gave them a temporary feeling of relief. They must have thought that since they would die soon from dehydration it didn't matter.

Only two things could save them: rescue or rainfall, and it had to happen within the next twenty-four to forty-eight hours.

That evening was exceptionally calm as it put an end to the searing heat of the day. Tony found evenings and early mornings a bit more tolerable because they were transition periods from temperature extremes, and for a brief time the temperature was comfortable.

Tony took his usual look at the sky, and again it was cloudless. He covered himself with as many rags of clothing as possible to ward off the oncoming chill of night. Closing his eyes, he tried not to the think that he only had a couple of days at most to live. The water would be gone tomorrow and sipping seawater would hasten his death.

About three hours after nightfall Tony got the surprise of his life. The skies opened up and pelted him with rain! Fresh, clear, cool, drenching rain. Nothing had ever felt so good!

Now the survivors had to capture that fresh water as fast as they could. The rain might stop at any moment.

Tony and others strong enough to move quickly gathered empty chocolate tins and laid them flat to catch the rain. They used the sail as a funnel to divert rain into the tins. Then they stood with mouths open and hands cupped and gulped down water as fast as possible.

Turning their attention to the men too weak to move, they held the water tins to their mouths. Tony was shocked to find that four of the men were too weak to even sip the water. Tony and the others did their best to hold the emaciated men's mouths open and dribble some water into them. A fifth man, named Upchurch, could barely drink and complained of a terrible headache.

The deluge of rain continued, and the four stronger men shouted for joy, sang, and laughed while drinking their fill. Soon they felt a bit of strength returning and rejoiced anew. The downpour washed the salt water from their skin, and that, too, felt wonderful.

Before the rain stopped they were able to fill both water cans, the empty bottles, and all the chocolate tins.

Despite the life-giving rain, the four weakest men died the next day, and the man named Upchurch passed away soon thereafter. That left four men in the lifeboat: Tony, Harry Vines, Ted Dobson, and Ted Riley. Both the Teds were able seamen in the

British navy, and both were in their twenties, which meant all four of the survivors were under thirty years of age.

Although the four people still alive in Tony's lifeboat had the good fortune of rain, they were even farther from shore than Jim and Doris's boat. But they were lucky; the rains now became somewhat predictable, raining approximately every other day. Survivors' skin, once painfully dry from the salt water and sun, was now supple. They could forget about water rations and drink as much as they wanted. And now that their mouths were no longer sore and parched, they could eat the biscuits, pemmican, and chocolate. The meager amount of food, however, only seemed to increase their hunger now that they had saliva in their mouths to chew and swallow.

Prior to the rains, the men lay silently, their tongues too swollen and dry to talk, but now they conversed frequently. Their primary topic of conversation, not surprisingly, focused on all the different types of food they would eat if they ever made it home. Ted Riley longed for a steak. Harry dreamed of sausages. Ted Dobson and Tony wanted pork pies like they enjoyed as boys. They spent hours crafting every serving of their dream dinners. All four of the young men also swore they would never waste water again, not even a single drop.

At night Tony and Harry huddled in the stern of the vessel, and the two Teds did the same in the bow. With extra clothing from the dead they made little tents to hold their warmth in. To protect them against the cold steel of the boat's hull they lay on life jackets.

Despite the rain and additional clothing, Tony didn't think they could stay alive until they reached landfall.

A COURAGEOUS WOMAN

JIM MCLOUGHLIN AND DORIS HAWKINS, LIFEBOAT #1

Approximately October 3–5

An albatross, a seabird with its giant ten-foot wingspan, soared above the lifeboat, which limped along under a tattered sail. It was now the first week of October, and Jim didn't think he could last more than a few days. He stared at the bird and thought of the Coleridge poem "Rime of the Ancient Mariner," which mentions an albatross. In that poem one line summed up Jim's plight perfectly: "Water, water, everywhere, / Nor any drop to drink."

Jim tried to take his mind off the salt water surrounding him and hoped the albatross would bring good luck. One of the survivors tried to catch fish with a hook crudely made from a biscuit tin attached to a piece of wire.

As Jim watched the fisherman try unsuccessfully to hook a fish, he was startled out of his lethargy when a whale suddenly surfaced next to the boat. Jim was eye to eye with the whale, and for a moment he forgot about his suffering, just looking at the magnificent animal. Perhaps the whale thought the lifeboat was another whale because it lingered alongside the vessel.

For a brief moment there was even humor on the boat when the fisherman said, "I caught us the biggest bloody fish you ever saw!"

"How are you going to get it on board?"

The fisherman had no answer.

Then the whale dove and its tail whacked the water so hard the boat rocked. Jim, Doris, and the others knew that if the tail had been just a little closer to the vessel, they would have capsized. It was their first lucky break in several days.

After treating so many people for their infected sores, Dr. Geoffrey Purslow had many of his own to deal with. His left hand and arm and his right foot and leg were infected, causing him great discomfort.

Doris pierced Dr. Purslow's finger to release the pus and cleaned the wound as best she could. But his swollen foot, when sliced, did not produce any discharge. Instead over the next few hours red streaks appeared on the doctor's leg and arm, indicating he was suffering from blood poisoning. His glands swelled, and the doctor could no longer help others. He lay quietly, knowing he did not have long to live.

Doris was enveloped by a deep sadness and told Jim the serious extent of the doctor's illness. There was nothing either of them could do.

A couple of days later the doctor made a courageous decision. He said to Doris and those around him, "As I cannot be of any further help, and now I am a source of danger to you all, it is better that I go." The doctor did not want to infect the other survivors.

He slowly inched his way up and sat on the gunwale.

Jim was trying to process what was happening.

The doctor gave a weak smile that Jim described as serene.

"Goodbye," said Dr. Purslow. He then let himself fall backward into the sea and was gone.

Jim was stunned. Doris, however, understood the doctor's self-sacrifice for what it was: his last desperate act to try to save others. There would be more water for the remaining survivors and no chance of them catching his infection.

Doris looked at Jim and said, "Greater love hath no man than to lay down his life for his friends."

The young doctor who had helped so many was now gone. It was an absolutely crushing blow for the group, especially Jim who had admired the way Dr. Purslow conducted himself throughout the ordeal. The doctor had survived approximately twenty days in the lifeboat only to take his own life to keep the others safe. It was all so sad that Jim was beyond crying.

Jim's resolve to fight on was gone. His thoughts were now on his own impending death, and he worried about the impact on his family. They wouldn't know what happened to him or how long he had kept up the struggle to live.

It was Doris who gave Jim the courage not to quit. She talked with him, encouraged him, and assured him they would be rescued. Instead of talking about death, Doris steered Jim to use his imagination and pretend they were sitting together for a friendly visit over a cup of tea.

"Milk and sugar in your tea?"

"Yes, thanks."

While Doris pretended to get the milk and sugar, Jim said he would first like a glass of water.

"Of course."

And the conversations went on and on, despite throats so dry they talked in whispers. The conversation did what Freckles intended, it roused Jim from his despair and renewed his hope.

Later Doris even revealed her own pain to Jim, explaining how she had been hired to bring a baby back to England on board the *Laconia*.

"I lost my grip on the dear little soul," Doris explained, "when I was going over the side. I have to survive this, McLoughlin."

She had to tell the child's family how she had been lost.

Jim thought, *What a courageous woman*. She showed him the way to keep fighting, by having that sense of purpose.

October 2 was Jim's twenty-first birthday. "This calls for a celebration," said Doris, still managing to stay upbeat. The water ration was given out early, and Jim received a double dose—two tablespoons.

That gesture meant the world to Jim. The few survivors left in the boat were honoring him with extra water while they remained at their usual amount. He asked Doris how much longer she thought they could keep going.

She smiled and said, "Awhile yet."

Jim wasn't so sure. Sixty-eight people had been in the boat at the start, and now only about half were still alive. And their supply of water was dangerously low.

Without water the end was near. It appeared that for all Doris's faith, nothing would save them.

PRECIOUS WATER

JIM MCLOUGHLIN AND DORIS HAWKINS, LIFEBOAT #1

Approximately October 5–6

Jim's suspicions that some of the men had thrown a few of the weaker ones overboard was confirmed one night. He heard a struggle near the stern of the boat, then the cries of a young sailor named Mickey, "No, I'm strong enough to pull an oar, please. I don't want to go overboard!"

There was a splash, followed by silence.

Jim sat in terror, forcing himself to stay awake all night long, worried he'd be next. He didn't know which men did this terrible act, so he trusted no one except Doris.

It seemed every time Jim thought things couldn't get worse they did. The death of Lady Grizel, the delirious man who started singing and kept singing even after he jumped overboard, the ship that passed but did not stop, Dr. Purslow's infection and death. What more could happen?

Jim and Doris soon found out. The drinking water ran out. This occurred about the twentieth day adrift in the lifeboat. Jim knew he was finished. Doris prayed for rain.

The next day it came! Not just a light rain but a tropical downpour. The survivors caught it in the biscuit tins and bailing tins and drank as fast as they could. Never had anything tasted so good. Their bodies absorbed the water like sponges. They shouted for joy at their good fortune. They took down the little sail and held it flat, letting the water pour from the sail into the empty water tank.

The rain continued for several hours, and the temperature kept dropping. They were wet and cold, but this time no one complained. The number of people in the boat had been reduced to sixteen, and Doris thought that if the rain had only come a week earlier many more would still be on board.

When the rain finally stopped around sunset, they had collected at least six gallons of precious water. The castaways spent a freezing, soggy night, many with earaches.

The next morning reality set in. Yes, they now had water to last awhile longer, but they were almost out of food and still had no idea how far they had to sail and drift before reaching Africa. And so they rationed the water, and endured another blazing hot day. Jim began to think the rain was just prolonging his suffering rather than bringing salvation.

SOMETHING IN THE DISTANCE

JIM MCLOUGHLIN AND DORIS HAWKINS, LIFEBOAT #1

October 7–9

The day after the rainfall Jim noticed that the color of the ocean was no longer a clear bluish green but instead had tinges of brown in it. He was too exhausted to try to understand the change. Then he saw a dragonfly, and a butterfly. His hopes soared; land could not be that far off.

Doris was observing the sky and water as well, and she noticed a gray gull, much smaller than the albatross they had seen. A leaf drifted by the boat in the ocean. She too became convinced land was near.

A day later cloud banks formed on the horizon and more bits of vegetation appeared in the water. Land had to be within a few miles, but still no sight of it.

October 8 was a clear day, and Jim saw dots on the horizon. Others stared in the same direction. No one could be sure what they were seeing, but several of the group guessed the dark marks might be ships.

Doris didn't dare say they were ships, nor did she wake any of the sleeping men. She didn't want to get everyone's hopes up only to have them squashed again should the ocean be playing tricks on them. The dots were not moving, as ships would. Over the next couple of hours the marks looked more like blotches, and they did appear to be a bit closer.

Jim began to see "sticks" coming up from the smudges and assumed they were a ship's masts. His hopes soared even higher.

Another half hour went by and they had their answer. The images on the horizon were not ships but land! The sticks were trees!

Those who comprehended what they were seeing cheered and woke up the sleeping.

The lifeboat drifted closer to land, and they began to make out hills and clearly see the trees. There were no signs of civilization, and they all wondered where they were. Extra rations of water were given out in celebration.

Night fell but no one could sleep with the anticipation of salvation. They thought by morning they might be close enough to row ashore. But the ocean wasn't done with them. At dawn an offshore breeze sprang up, and instead of getting closer to land they watched the hills and trees get smaller and smaller. All they could do was wait and hope they would be found. Sea birds squawked above them, as if mocking these half-dead humans.

The waiting was unbearable for Jim. They had been so close to land that even the air smelled different.

Late in the day, the wind changed and pushed them in the direction of the land, which they knew must be Africa. Then, late in the day, when they were about five miles out from shore a plane approached. The British Union Jack was painted on its body.

Survivors who had the energy waved, trying desperately to attract the pilot's attention.

When the plane was directly overhead, it banked hard, an indication the pilot had seen them. Finally, Doris and Jim shed tears of joy, not bitter disappointment.

The plane circled above, coming lower and lower. The pilot opened the window and waved a white handkerchief. He did not have any containers of water to drop, so he did the next best thing. He had one of his airmen write "O.K. Help coming" on a life jacket, and attach it to a linen bag with some fruit inside. Then, when they were directly above the lifeboat, the airmen tossed it all out the window.

The pilot was Captain A. G. Storrs, and he later wrote in his report, "We circled for some time but could find no container in which water could be dropped. So we filled a double pillow slip with fresh fruit, a can of orange juice, and a waterproof bag containing cigarettes, matches and a note. To this pack was tied one of the life jackets. A bombing run was made over the boat, and the bundle dropped."

The life jacket landed close to the boat, but the bag broke apart and the fruit drifted in different directions. A man from the stern risked going overboard to get the life jacket and whatever fruit he could grab. He snatched an apple, pear, and banana, along with the life jacket, and returned to the boat.

Reading the words "O.K. Help coming" was even more powerful and welcome than the rainfall:

their ordeal was near its end. Also on the life jacket were more scrawled words: "You are 60 miles south of Monrovia."

The survivors didn't know where Monrovia was, nor did they care; they just wanted a ship or plane that could land on water to come and rescue them.

Monrovia is part of Liberia, where West Africa juts out into the Atlantic. Had their lifeboat drifted in a more northerly direction, they might have missed Africa altogether and still been far out at sea. It was a lucky break after all the bad ones.

The survivors looked back toward land and could see spray flung into the air where the waves met the rocky coast. The last thing they needed now was to drift too close to that cauldron of breaking seas. The booming sound of breaking waves reached all the way to the lifeboat, which was now about a mile or two offshore.

A breeze was pushing them in the direction of the rocks. Jim, despite wanting desperately to be on land and out of the miserable lifeboat, didn't like the looks of the shoreline.

Another survivor surveyed the shore. "I think there's a beach!" He pointed to one area where the waves didn't crash or send spray upward, explaining that must be an area with sand rather than rock. Jim and Doris hoped he was correct, knowing that the wind was pushing them in that direction and they hadn't the strength to row away. As far as they could see in both directions, were rock cliffs where waves exploded, except for that one little area of shoreline that was calmer than the rest. If their boat landed anywhere but there, they were doomed.

The man on the tiller guided the boat as best he could toward the calm area. No one spoke. Their lives now depended on his ability to steer. The booming got louder, but everyone on board kept their eyes on the tranquil spot where they could see a sandy beach surrounded by jungle.

Big rolling waves propelled them forward, their speed increasing with each passing second. This was the time for silent prayers. After all they had been through, it was too terrible to think they might capsize and drown in the crashing seas or be hurled against the rocks.

A wave sent them surfing toward shore at an alarming pace.

"We're going in!" the man on the tiller shouted. There was no other option. He tried to point the bow at the sand. Jim, Doris, and the others hung on to gunwales or anything fixed to the boat for fear of being swept away.

Suddenly the boat came to a grinding halt as it hit a sandbar. A following wave slammed the vessel sending it sideways. The next wave propelled the bow high and then put the vessel on its side, spilling its occupants out like flotsam.

Flung out of the boat, the survivors held their breath as they fell into the sea. A wave tumbled Jim and the others like logs through shallow water, their skin scraping the sand. As the wave receded they began crawling to shore before the next wave dragged them out.

They continued crawling until they emerged from the ocean that had held them hostage for so many days. Then they collapsed, panting on the sand like injured fish hurled onto the shore.

It was October 9. They had been in the open boat for twenty-four days. These sixteen souls, out of the original sixty-eight, had drifted seven hundred miles.

STILL AT SEA

TONY LARGE, LIFEBOAT #2

Approximately October 9–20

WHILE JIM AND DORIS HAD FINALLY REACHED LAND, Tony and the survivors in his lifeboat were still over a hundred miles away.

Besides having plenty of water, Tony felt fortunate to have Harry Vines in his lifeboat. Harry proved to be the best seaman and was quite handy. When the boom on their jury-rigged sail broke, it was Harry who fixed it without any tools. Tony marveled at Harry's practicality and inventiveness, and the two men's friendship deepened as they discussed all sorts of subjects. But one morning Harry woke up and not only wouldn't speak, he refused both food and drink while avoiding eye contact with any of the survivors. He simply stared off at the horizon.

Tony was alarmed, especially after his friend Canada let the ocean take his life. The morning passed, and Tony tried coaxing Harry to talk or at least explain what had caused the sudden change in the man who had been so steady and inspiring. Harry stayed silent and withdrawn. *Would he too take his own life? Had Harry suddenly reached the breaking point?*

Then the dark curtain of his temporary depression lifted, and during the afternoon he was back to his old self. Mood swings in a lifeboat after weeks adrift with little hope of survival should not have surprised Tony. He certainly had his highs and lows, with the lows harder to bounce back from as time went on. Although the survivors now had water, they had no idea where they were, nor any sign of a ship since the close call with the freighter.

Staring at the same companions day after day often resulted in tension between the men. Tony frequently whistled to pass the time even though he knew it got on the nerves of his fellow survivors. He in turn was agitated by Ted Dobson's constant combing and stroking of his beard. The hostility never came to blows because they needed each other to survive and were much too weak to waste energy on something foolish. They had to conserve their strength for periodic bailing of the boat because the rains came more frequently, often as long tropical downpours. The men now looked forward to sunny periods despite the oppressive heat and humidity. The sun meant a chance to dry out their soggy garments and their little makeshift tents.

Two days after Harry had gone into his funk, one of the Teds exploded in rage and frustration, shouting he couldn't take any more. He said he was going to swim away from the boat. Harry used a bit of reverse psychology to get Ted to think about what he was doing.

Instead of pleading with Ted not to jump overboard, Harry said that Ted should leave his wristwatch in the vessel and then throw himself into the sea. That would mean more rations for the other three. The two men hollered at each other and then collapsed in exhaustion, out of breath from the exertion of the emotional exchange. It was a bitter altercation, but Harry's rebuke and challenge to Ted worked. Ted stayed with the boat and soon calmed himself.

Tony found solace and hope in a "divine presence" and a feeling that something more powerful than himself was guiding him. He had survived the initial sinking of the *Laconia*. He then eluded sharks, barracudas, and the American bombs, and was outlasting starvation and dehydration. Tony did not view his survival as luck or fate. He considered how many unusual events had increased his chance for survival. Chief among them was the help from the very submarine that sank his ship and how it rained just when their water ran out. To Tony, these instances were clear evidence of a higher power. While he couldn't understand exactly what that higher force was all about or why he was chosen to be alive while others perished, Tony nevertheless trusted his belief that he was not alone.

On October 20 Tony heard a most welcome sound, even if for only a moment. The drone of an engine made him look up for a plane, but there were too many clouds to see very far. He wondered whether they were getting close to land. Birds different from the one or two species he'd seen days earlier seemed to confirm this. A patch of oil in the water proved they were nearer to mankind. And two days after hearing the first plane, the survivors saw another, although the pilot gave no indication he had seen the lifeboat.

Tony was a tense bundle of nerves; they simply had to be found before their food gave out or before one of the remaining four died. The anticipation that maybe, just maybe, they would be found kept them alert and on edge, but as the night of October 20 turned into the early morning hours of October 21, there was no sound of a rescue ship or plane approaching. The night passed agonizingly slow.

At dawn, Tony crawled out of his shelter. In the gray light he could see far enough to gauge that there was no ship nearby. But something unusual caught his eye. Far away was a smudge on the northern horizon that looked to be solid, and not fog. Tony woke up Harry, and he too saw the mark on the horizon. Hopes soared, but then the smudge disappeared. It was yet another bitter blow, and Tony lay back down in his shelter. His knee had become infected and swollen, and even the slightest movement hurt.

Harry kept scanning the ocean in all directions. After a short time he squinted—there was the solid object again. As he stared, he thought he could make out dark little sticks against the sky. He called to Tony, "Get out quickly! Come and look!"

Tony groaned and once again emerged from the shelter. This time there was no mistake. He could see the pinpoints on the horizon and saw tiny streams of smoke. He knew he was looking at a ship's masts and funnels belching smoke. A convoy of ships!

The two men could only pray that if they could see the ships, the sailors on those vessels could see them too. But that would be a long shot, as their lifeboat only rose a few feet above the surface of the ocean. A dark storm cloud was approaching, and that threatened to obscure the visibility.

Tony decided not to wake the two Teds. He and Harry could make out the ship's rough shapes. One vessel signaled another with its lamp. It looked as if one of the ships was turning. But which way? Was it coming toward the castaways or heading in the opposite direction? The two survivors could not tell from such a distance, but they could no longer sit still. Tony got to his feet and waved a blue shirt wildly over his head, the pain of his swollen knee forgotten.

The ship that turned was an escort, steaming at the edge of the convoy to protect the bigger vessels from U-boats. A lookout on the escort ship saw something in the distance, and he assumed it was a conning tower of a U-boat just breaking the ocean's surface. He shouted the alarm. The navy sailors sprinted to their battle stations as the ship raced toward what it thought was the U-boat, prepared to sink it.

What the lookout had seen was not a U-boat, but the lifeboat holding the last four survivors of the *Laconia*!

Tony could see the small escort ship speeding their way. This was no mirage! He woke up the two Teds, calling for them to come out of their shelter, a ship was coming!

One of the Teds had had enough with the close encounters of ships and planes not seeing the lifeboat. "Don't joke about things like that," he said sourly.

Tony shouted back that this time it was for real. The ship was coming right at them. (At the time it never occurred to Tony that the ship was coming to blast away at an imagined U-boat.)

The survivors could now see that the escort ship was British, and it circled the lifeboat in a wide arc, making sure no U-boats were lurking nearby, afraid that the lifeboat was part of some deadly trick.

The escort ship soon stopped just upwind of the

lifeboat and drifted toward it. The four survivors knew for sure they were saved!

They gathered the tattered possessions they had collected from those who died (watches, wallets, identity tags from the military men, and other odd belongings) and their lone book, a Bible. So concerned were they about food that they even packed up what was left of the chocolate and pemmican.

The castaways said a quick prayer of thanks and started "chattering like men bereft of their senses and laughing with happiness."

Sailors from the ship came down a ladder to help the survivors climb up into the vessel. A crowd of sailors stared at them in amazement as the four survivors hugged one another while laughing and crying at the same time.

Down below, bobbing on the gray ocean, the steel lifeboat that had kept them alive drifted away.

The name of their savior ship was *St. Wistan*. Its convoy was headed to Freetown, just a day's journey away. They were still one hundred miles from land, even though the castaways had drifted seven hundred miles. These four lone survivors were lucky indeed to have been found.

Part V

POST-RESCUE

KIND, COMPASSIONATE PEOPLE

JIM MCLOUGHLIN AND DORIS HAWKINS, LIBERIA

Approximately October 9 into December

ALTHOUGH JIM, DORIS, AND THE OTHERS FROM their lifeboat were on land, the ground felt as if it were rocking due to the many days at sea. Their legs felt useless, like brittle sticks.

Jim tried to stand but toppled over and could not get up. The sand painfully scraped his sores, and the leg with the barracuda bite throbbed. How would they ever be able to walk to find help?

The lifeboat was tossed onto the beach a few seconds after the survivors washed ashore. A couple of the stronger men crawled to it and removed the remaining food and water. Night began closing in on the sixteen shipwrecked castaways, and they huddled for safety and warmth. They worried about wild animals in the dense jungle behind them.

None of the survivors felt strong enough to even attempt to start walking.

In the darkening evening, the emaciated and exhausted survivors saw a light coming through the jungle. Doris and Jim stared into the trees with a mix of trepidation and hope. Would the people be friend or foe?

Two of the survivors managed to stagger toward the jungle. Seconds later a group of villagers appeared. Some had tattoos and white paint on their black skin. The leader put his arms around the two survivors and in broken English said, "Thank God you are safe." Then the rest of the villagers greeted all the survivors. In a mix of English and their own native tongue, they were able to communicate that they had been watching the lifeboat for the past two days. (The villagers lived near a trading town and some had learned English.) They had expected to find the lifeboat wrecked and the passengers dead, but now were overjoyed that they had survived.

"Two days [we] cry for you in the village," explained the leader. Now finding that the boat people had somehow made it to shore and through the surf alive, the villagers all laughed and some even danced.

Doris and Jim did the opposite. Their emotions caused them to sob like babies. The relief they felt was too much to keep bottled inside. And the compassion shown by these local people further moved the survivors to tears after so much hardship and trauma.

One of the survivors asked where they were, and the locals answered Liberia.

Later Doris found out that some of the villagers were descendants of American emancipated slaves who had returned to their African homeland.

The villagers explained that they would take the castaways to their homes. They helped up those who had the strength to stand and supported them on the walk up the hill and through the tangle of trees and vines. Jim and some others were so close to death that they could not stand and were carried. He was grateful when a villager picked him up like an "empty sack."

Doris was too weak to walk far on her wobbly legs, and she received a piggyback ride for part of the trek through the jungle. The humidity increased the farther they traveled from the coast, and the walk to the village seemed to take forever. Jim and Doris desperately needed rest, but also food and water. But they let their guides carry them onward.

Finally Jim could see a clearing ahead. Small cooking fires lighted thatched huts arranged in a semicircle.

A bunch of villagers were standing by one of the larger shelters. When they got a good look at the survivors, some cried; others laughed with happiness that the castaways were alive; and a few just stared. There were children too, shy and wide-eyed at these sickly people from another land.

The large shelter was a communal hut with a roof but no walls, and the survivors were led inside. And then, to their delight, they were served coconut milk, oranges, bananas, and other fruit. But the survivors had been without food so long, and their tongues were so swollen and sore, that it was difficult to swallow, and they ate very little.

Doris was initially mistaken for a man. Her hair

was matted and tangled, and her emaciated body was clothed only in the tattered remnants of army shorts and an air force shirt. It wasn't until one of the female villagers noticed Doris had no beard that a group of women approached and asked whether she was a woman. When she said yes, the women put their hands up in dismay—now they truly understood what Doris had been through.

Jim felt peace come over him as the castaways slept in the communal hut that night. In the morning three of the stronger survivors were taken to a nearby town, Grand Bassa, where a handful of Dutch and Syrians lived. Those who could not walk, including Jim and Doris, were carried down to the beach where they had washed ashore. Soon native canoes with sails arrived, and the survivors were loaded on board. Jim was nervous about going back on the ocean in any kind of vessel, let alone a canoe made from a hollowed-out tree trunk.

Despite Jim's misgivings, the canoe was seaworthy, and he and Doris were ferried to Grand Bassa and rejoined the others. The people of Grand Bassa were shocked at how pitiful the starved survivors looked, and many started to cry. Jim cried too and found that over the next few days he would inexplicably break into tears.

Small groups of survivors were taken to individual homes. Townspeople showed their compassion and generosity, carefully bathing the castaways, giving them new clothing, and helping them into beds with clean sheets. Healing ointment was put on their many sores. Ever so slowly they began to eat. Jim found he did best on a diet of Quaker oats, fruit, and milk. Unfortunately, one of the surviving sixteen developed an infection and a fever that continued to climb. He was so weak that his body could not properly fight back and he died. How tragic that after all those days adrift he passed away just two days after being rescued.

While Jim gradually improved physically, his mental state was one of confusion. He was unable to read, carry on much of a conversation, or focus in general. In his words, he still "felt lost." Doris seemed to recover more quickly than Jim.

On October 25 the survivors were put on a small ship bound for Freetown. They had only been on the ship for a few hours when the submarine alert siren sounded and men rushed to battle stations. Jim and

Doris were a bundle of raw nerves. *Not again* went through their minds.

Despite the alarm, they made it to Freetown safely. Here the survivors were questioned by British military officials and told to keep quiet about the American plane bombing U-156. The whole truth about the deaths of *Laconia* passengers wouldn't be revealed for decades, when US military officials commissioned a report about it.

They said goodbye to one another as they would be assigned different ships for transport home. The separation happened so quickly that Jim and Freckles only had a chance for a quick goodbye, with Doris saying, "We won't forget our little journey in a hurry."

Doris steamed off on a cargo ship. It was a "nightmare" journey of great anxiety as the ship traveled unescorted and could fall prey to a U-boat at any time. A gale during voyage battered the vessel with great waves. "Every bang," she said, "made me leap from my bunk." But the ship did make it to England, and Doris was home on December 18.

Jim did not heal as well as Doris, and he was taken to a hospital ship in Freetown harbor. He was quite ill, with a fever of 105. Malaria had struck him. Would he be like the other survivor who had stayed alive for weeks at sea, only to succumb after making it safely to land?

Jim fought the shivers, shakes, and delirium for many days. The symptoms would abate for a day or two, only to come roaring back again. He was so sick that he was not allowed to board the ship he was scheduled to take back to England. He was devastated; he only wanted to see his family again.

This turn of events proved to be a lucky break: the ship he was supposed to take was sunk by a U-boat!

Because Jim was in the Royal Navy, he was soon assigned as a crew member on another ship, where he was expected to work as hard as the other men. He wondered how in the world he could do that after his illness and weeks of malnutrition and dehydration. But he didn't argue; he just wanted to go home.

And finally he did make it home after many storm-filled days at sea. He arrived just in time for Christmas. His sisters and parents were astonished when he knocked on their door. The British Admiralty had told them that Jim was lost at sea, and they assumed he was dead. But Jim was very much alive.

He had survived the cruelties of both war and the unforgiving ocean, and now he set out on another journey to begin his life anew.

Doris and Jim exchanged letters, but they never saw each other in person again. Both wondered why they survived the *Laconia* when so many did not. But one thing was certain: during their time in the lifeboat they had shown compassion, kindness, and courage.

AT LAST

TONY LARGE

October 20 into December

THE CREW OF THE *ST. WISTAN* SHOWED TONY AND the other three survivors every kindness. While the castaways drank tea loaded with sugar, the ship's crew peppered them with questions, astonished that the four men had somehow stayed alive with so little food and water. The sailors couldn't help but gawk at the four skeletal men and wanted to know how they had survived. The two Teds and Harry had long shaggy beards, but Tony, who was just nineteen, had only stubble. One of the sailors on the ship wanted to know how he managed to shave each day! Tony could only laugh—the lifeboat didn't even contain a knife, let alone a razor.

They were given food, but their shrunken stomachs could only handle a small amount. Only bread with jam seemed to agree with them. They were served small portions at frequent intervals, and they slowly regained strength. They were so relieved to be safe that they often found themselves singing and whistling, but the sailors quickly informed them that no whistling was allowed. A maritime superstition holds that whistling brings bad luck and bad weather. Tony stopped whistling—he had had enough pain from the ocean and the war, and he wasn't going to tempt fate. U-boats were still prowling off the coast of Africa.

The survivors bathed, had their sores and wounds attended to, and even received haircuts. They had formed such a bond through their ordeal, that now, even though they were rescued, they stayed together. Despite their rescuers' attentions, Tony knew that only the two Teds and Harry could truly understand what he was thinking or feeling. The four castaways had no interest in learning about what was happening in the world or with the war. Their world revolved around food, water, and one another. It would take considerable time for them to show more than a passing interest in issues beyond that.

Like those in Doris and Jim's lifeboat, the men were warned by government officials to keep quiet about the B-24 bombers that tried to sink U-156 and U-506. An American government official who spoke to those who survived weeks in lifeboats told his superiors, "When the entire story of this episode [is] written I am confident it will survive as one of the most heart-rending stories of the war."

After a brief stay at a hospital in Freetown, the men boarded a ship for Great Britain. Once the ship reached port, they said heartfelt goodbyes and went their separate ways. They all arrived home in time for Christmas, and then did their best to put their ordeal behind them and live normal lives.

That, however, was impossible after being so close to death for so long. They had survived on the lifeboat for an astounding thirty-five days. Adding to their stress, was that all four men were still in the navy and had to go back to sea.

A year later, Tony had a most memorable and

meaningful encounter with another lifeboat survivor: Doris Hawkins. He found her a remarkable and delightful woman, who knew exactly the kind of inner turmoil still roiling inside him. Both wondered why they survived when so many others in their lifeboats had perished. It was a question neither of them would ever be able to answer.

PRISON

CLAUDE PARR, MOLLY DAVIDSON, AND JOSEPHINE FRAME, CASABLANCA

September and October 1942

On the Vichy French ship *Gloire*, Claude Parr worried that he could be held prisoner for months. He was kept in a large holding cell with the other men as the vessel steamed toward Africa. He was given food and water and allowed a shower, but his captors would not tell him his fate.

Josephine and Molly, also on the *Gloire*, fared better than the British men, but their ordeal was far from over. It was sweltering hot on the ship, which made people listless and tired. They were too numb to be curious about where the French were taking them.

Since their names and addresses had been recorded, they hoped their families would be notified through the Red Cross that they were still alive.

Three days of travel brought the ship to Dakar, a port in French West Africa. Everyone watched with guarded optimism when the captain went ashore to confer with authorities, but the hope didn't last long.

"Are we getting off here?" Josephine Frame asked her father.

"They said no, there's too much yellow fever," he replied.

Not getting off in Dakar prolonged everyone's discomfort and just delayed the inevitable. The Vichy French were officially neutral but known to collaborate with the Germans, so the *Laconia* survivors were going to be prisoners of war no matter where they ended up. They could only hope for tolerable conditions. Comfort and enjoyment seemed far in the past.

Josephine took younger kids under her wing, keeping them busy with games, stories, and songs. She tried to hold despair at bay, telling herself that showers and regular rations of food aboard the ship were more than a step above what she'd experienced in the lifeboats.

At night Molly Davidson slept on a hard tabletop while her mother curled up on the floor underneath. They were worried about being put in a prison camp wherever the ship finally docked, but they did their best just to be thankful to be alive.

A week after rounding up the survivors, the *Gloire* sailed around the Ivory Coast and arrived in Casablanca, Morocco, on the northwest coast of the African continent. It was a relief for Molly and Josephine to see trees and buildings instead of the sea. But when the gangplank was lowered, British women and children were ordered into trucks. The four hundred or so Italian POWs left the ship next. Even though they were not going to prison camps, they appeared downcast. They were likely to be sent back to fight against the Allies in the desert.

Claude and the other British and Polish men were led off the ship under armed guard. They were put on trucks just as crowded as the lifeboat, with no room to sit. Claude knew he was being taken to a prison camp and wondered whether his treatment would take a turn for the worse.

The prison was run by Vichy French, and the camp was surrounded by barbed wire and watchtowers manned by machine gun–toting guards. Claude saw there was little chance to escape. He was put into a hut with forty other men. There were no beds or blankets, just piles of straw to sleep on. The food rations were meager, and the food itself was terrible: pea soup with pieces of rotting horsemeat floating in it and a piece of bread given out twice a day.

Molly, Josephine, and the other British women and children were brought to a smaller camp where conditions were slightly better. Food was scarce and tasteless, usually consisting of an egg and coffee for breakfast, then a thin lentil and artichoke soup at dinner. Lice and bedbugs infested the straw bedding, and the single blanket issued to each person wasn't any defense against them. Bathrooms consisted of open pit latrines that everyone avoided as much as possible. Josephine's family, who were able to stay together in one large room of a hut, adopted a gecko that ate mosquitoes and were grateful for its presence.

"There was a Swedish girl in the camp," Molly remembered. "I don't know why she was there, but she said she'd go into town and tell the British consul that we were there."

Similarly, Josephine met a German woman who

was a professor whose presence in the camp was a mystery, but these fellow prisoners offered the *Laconia* survivors important pieces of information that helped them get along.

There was an uprising among prisoners at Josephine's camp, where a few male prisoners worked in the kitchen. After preparing the same soup of lentils and artichokes day after day for weeks, the British men had rebelled, throwing a day's supply of artichokes over the prison wall to send a message that they wanted some variety. Guards threw the artichokes back at the prisoners, who complied and got back to making soup.

Women with money could request a pass to go into town to supplement their meager diet. Molly's mother had some money tucked away, so she purchased a small charcoal stove and some potatoes. The women and children adjusted to a daily routine of waiting for news. Molly's mother recorded events in a diary, and Josephine continued to gather younger children for lessons and games despite having no books and few resources like paper and pencils.

More clothing was made available when the British ambassador alerted the Red Cross that civilian women and children were present in the camps. The Red Cross also provided a financial allowance and helped prisoners send letters home. Writing letters home helped relieve the monotony and discomfort of the prison camp, but Molly and Josephine started to doubt that they would ever be free.

Chapter 32

LONG ROAD TO FREEDOM

CLAUDE PARR, MOLLY DAVIDSON, AND JOSEPHINE FRAME

November 1942–March 1943

Claude and the men languished in the prison camp until early November. One night he was awakened to distant booms and thought a thunderstorm was heading his way. He fell back to sleep. When morning dawned and he stepped outside, his eyes widened. The guards were gone!

Not a single guard was patrolling the perimeter of the fence, nor was anyone in the watchtowers. Cautiously Claude walked into the sunlight and realized the large gate into the prison compound was open.

Claude and the others weren't sure what to do. Should they run away? But if they ran, where would they be safe in North Africa? And why had the guards left?

They had their answer just a couple of hours later. Planes were coming toward them. The men squinted into the sun, praying these were not Nazi aircraft. A cheer went up when they saw the American insignia on the wings. The situation was now clear; the Allies had invaded North Africa. The booming sounds they heard the night before were not thunder but bombs being dropped by the Allies on German military installations. The guards knew that American and British troops would soon be coming and had fled.

Claude and the other prisoners ran back into their huts and emerged with armloads of hay. In the prison yard they arranged the hay to spell out POW. They wanted the pilots to know who they were, to make sure they were rescued and not mistakenly bombed.

The planes overhead were part of Operation Torch, a three-pronged attack to gain control of the Vichy French territories in North Africa. While the campaign was successful in about a week, the outcome was uncertain during the first few days. (The

Vichy French forces put up stiff resistance until it was clear they would be defeated, and their leaders made a deal to cooperate with the Allies.)

A few of the prisoners started walking to Casablanca, but Claude and a majority of the men thought it was best to stay where they were and hope rescue was on the way. Soon some of the Vichy French guards returned in trucks and treated the prisoners differently, perhaps knowing that the Allies would soon be arriving. They told the prisoners that they would take them to another prison camp where they would be safe from the fighting and soon set free. Claude decided to trust them.

The prisoners were loaded onto trucks and taken to the docks at Casablanca, where they were greeted by a wonderful sight. A US Navy ship, the *Ancon*, was waiting for them. They were free men, but they weren't going home just yet. Claude was told the only way for him to eventually get to Britain was via the *Ancon*, which was traveling to the United States first. He felt he had no choice but to board the ship if he wanted to leave Africa and eventually make it home.

Fortunately, Molly and Josephine had better luck. Soon American troops arrived to inspect their prison camp. The Allies had been victorious invading Morocco and were moving east toward Algiers, hoping to establish a foothold in North Africa before attacking the Axis forces fighting in Libya and Egypt. They were surprised to find British prisoners, particularly civilians like Josephine's family, Molly, and her mother. The Americans brought better food but told everyone to stay put a little longer while transportation was arranged.

Within a week Molly, Josephine, and the others arrived in Gibraltar, the tiny British territory on Spain's southern Mediterranean coast. Traveling on the hospital ship *Newfoundland*, they discarded the ragged and dirty clothing they had been wearing since *Laconia* was torpedoed. Freshly cleaned, their hair cut, and wearing new clothes, they began to put the awful chapter of the sinking behind them.

Josephine's nightly prayer to be home by Christmas became a reality. Due to the dangers German submarines still posed, they traveled from Gibraltar aboard SS *Ormonde* in a heavily armed convoy arriving in Liverpool on December 3, 1942.

The 102-day ordeal was finally over for Molly and Josephine.

For Claude, getting back home would take even longer. Claude and some of the other male survivors sailed to Norfolk, Virginia. Then they were put on a train bound for New York City. The men went from the heat of Casablanca to the bitter cold of a northeastern winter in the United States. Claude wasn't complaining. He was fed well and given warm clothes.

Claude heard about a ship sailing to Britain and joined the crew of the Dutch cargo ship *Salawati* as a steward. On December 13 Claude started the voyage back home. The ship traveled in a convoy for protection and steamed in a zigzag pattern to make it more difficult for a U-boat to sink it. Claude was nervous about another U-boat attack, especially since the *Salawati*'s cargo was ammunition for the war effort. If a torpedo should hit the ship, it would blow sky high, with no hope of survival.

The voyage went well until bad weather hit. A giant wave slammed the *Salawati* and washed the ship's second officer off the deck. Crew members heard him shouting for help in the waves behind the stern, but the ship was in danger from the massive seas. If the captain turned the ship to rescue the man overboard, he risked having the vessel capsize. So they had to leave the officer to a terrible fate.

Because of damage sustained during the bad weather, the *Salawati* headed for a closer port than England, and instead went to St. John's in Newfoundland. Here the captain became seriously ill. Claude wondered if he'd ever make it home as he waited for a new captain to take command. Icy winter winds with blasts of snow made the stay in Newfoundland all the more uncomfortable.

Finally in March 1943, Claude arrived home. The long nightmare that started on the *Laconia* was over.

EPILOGUE

U-156 AND COMMANDER HARTENSTEIN

Commander Werner Hartenstein and fifty-two crewmen were in U-156 in the Atlantic Ocean just east of the Caribbean island of Barbados when a US Navy "flying boat" bombed the submarine on May 8, 1943. The aircrew reported that the vessel split in half and sunk. About five members of the sub's crew were seen alive and swimming to a rubber raft but were never found.

In addition to the *Laconia*, U-156 sank nineteen ships and damaged four more, including the USS *Blakely*, an American destroyer that had also been used in World War I.

After the war Hartenstein's legacy as a humanitarian

grew, and annual gatherings were held in his hometown of Plauen, Germany, to commemorate the actions of Hartenstein and his crew following the *Laconia* sinking.

U-506 AND COMMANDER WÜRDEMANN

On July 12, 1943, an American anti-submarine B-24 aircraft found U-506 sitting on the surface of the ocean about three hundred miles off Spain. The crew was changing the submarine's batteries, which took longer than expected. Despite cloudy conditions the aircraft identified the submarine through radar and swooped down, dropping seven bombs that broke the U-boat's outer shell. Just a few men on the conning tower managed to escape. Commander Erich Würdemann was among them, but he did not have a life jacket and appeared injured. He told his crew to fend for themselves before slipping below the waves. Six managed to climb into a life raft dropped from the Liberator. They were rescued several days later by a British destroyer.

Würdemann's U-boat sank fifteen ships and was at sea for a total of 344 days on four patrols before it met its demise.

U-507 AND COMMANDER SCHACHT

Commander Harro Schacht and his crew returned to the Brazilian coast in December 1942 and sank three ships by early January 1943. The success they experienced was familiar, as they had sunk six ships off Brazil in August 1942, prompting the country to declare war against Germany.

This time things would be different. On January 8, a US plane dropped bombs on U-507, killing all on board. The loss of U-507 and the decorated commander in January 1943 was an indication that the war in the Atlantic was beginning to favor the Allies. This experienced captain had sunk nineteen ships totaling more than 75,000 GRT since taking command of his vessel just a year earlier.

TONY LARGE

On October 10, 1942, the parents of Tony Large were notified by telegram that their son was "lost at sea" in the sinking of the *Laconia*. About ten days later they received another telegram, from Tony himself, briefly assuring them that he had arrived in Africa intact. His older brother Peter wasn't so lucky, as he was killed by a German bullet in Normandy in 1944.

After the war Tony attended medical school at Guy's Hospital in London, then practiced in Durban, South Africa, for several years. He and his family moved to Tasmania, an island near Melbourne, Australia, where he was a busy and deeply appreciated "country doctor" who made house calls. He had three children and called his home *St. Wistan* after the trawler that found his lifeboat. The bell from the trawler that rescued him hung outside his house.

In 2001, he published *In Deep and Troubled Waters*, his first-person account of the *Laconia* sinking and his experience aboard the lifeboat. The book satisfied his desire to document the episode but caused him nightmares, according to his family. Tony died in 2017.

DORIS HAWKINS

Writing about the *Laconia* incident became a mission for Doris Hawkins when she returned home. The British National Archives has many letters she wrote to officials, trying to help sort out details of the ordeal. She identified people she knew had died trying to get from U-156 to the lifeboats when the American plane dropped bombs.

Doris also wrote letters to and visited the families of many who perished in the lifeboats she was in. In addition, she sought awards for those who showed selfless courage through the ordeal, including Dr. Geoffrey Purslow. In 1943 Doris published her account of the events in a booklet called *Atlantic Torpedo*. From 1948 to 1971 she worked at the British Hospital for Mothers and Babies in Woolwich, England. She died in 1991.

MOLLY DAVIDSON

When she returned to England from her perilous passage across the Atlantic, Molly aimed to make a difference in the war effort. She was one of 640,000 British women to join the military for service mostly within the country. Healthy, able-bodied men were scarce for many jobs during wartime so women were trained to fill in. Their jobs included building ships, repairing and test-flying military aircraft, and operating sensitive military strategies and communications. Molly Davidson joined the Women's Royal

Naval Service at Scapa Flow, a critically important naval base in Scotland. After the war Molly settled down with her husband, Fred Lewes, and raised four children in Exeter, England. She stayed in touch with several *Laconia* survivors but rarely spoke in public about her experience. She died in 2000.

JOSEPHINE FRAME

Selected to attend college, Josephine became a math teacher and school administrator while raising two daughters. She later helped to run a family-owned company and traveled extensively. Long after the war Josephine wanted to show her appreciation of U-156 Commander Werner Hartenstein's humane gesture. She traveled to his hometown of Plauen, Germany. An organization called the International Submarine Connection was formed there to recognize Hartenstein's actions. Josephine traveled to Germany five times, each time spending a week speaking to students about her experiences and about Hartenstein's role. She also helped to unveil a plaque honoring Hartenstein in the church he attended in Plauen. She held public talks to community groups about her wartime experiences until she was in her mid-nineties.

JIM MCLOUGHLIN

Although Jim frequently experienced terrible nightmares about his ordeal, he lived a good life with his wife, Dorothy. They had three children and moved to Adelaide, Australia, where he had a career as a police officer and detective. He contacted and corresponded with several other *Laconia* survivors, including Tony Large, and wrote a memoir called *One Common Enemy*. Jim died in 2013.

CLAUDE PARR

After the war Claude married, and he and his wife, Winifred, decided that he would leave the Merchant Navy, where he had worked on commercial ships like the *Laconia* and *Salawati*. They settled and had three children in the village of Burwell, England. His stories eventually inspired his grandson, Gavin Parr, to compile them into a book called *A Seemingly Ordinary Man*.

JAMES D. HARDEN

The B-24 Liberator crew that dropped bombs on U-156 and U-506 continued to fly missions throughout the Mediterranean region. The plane they used to bomb U-156 crashed in Palestine in October 1942 as Lt. Harden and his crew were on their way to join the 343rd Bombardment Squadron in the Middle East. The men survived. In 1943, they were awarded medals for sinking U-156 and U-506; officials learned later that neither submarine had been fully destroyed. Harden returned to his native Oklahoma to raise a family after the war. His obituary said he had been awarded the Distinguished Flying Cross during the war. A film crew interviewed him about the *Laconia* incident in the 1990s, and he appeared to regret dropping bombs on U-156. He died in 1998.

ROBERT C. RICHARDSON III

The young captain who ordered Harden to drop bombs on U-156 had a long military career, eventually becoming a general. He defended his order to attack U-156 by saying it was strategically justified because submarines were not recognized as rescue ships. Richardson denied that there was any cover-up of the bombing by an American plane, saying that those who sought information about it simply asked the wrong people. Richardson died in 2011.

KARL DÖNITZ

At the end of World War II, Adolf Hitler surprised everyone by naming Admiral Dönitz as his successor. Following Hitler's suicide, Dönitz oversaw Germany's surrender to the Allies.

Dönitz was one of very few high-ranking Germans to avoid the death penalty in the war crime trials at Nuremberg, Germany. He was questioned about his involvement in human rights abuses carried out by Nazis as well as the Laconia Order, which forbade submarine crews from aiding shipwreck survivors. When American Admiral Chester Nimitz admitted that the US Navy had a similar policy of refusing aid to shipwreck survivors, Dönitz was spared. He served ten years in Berlin's Spandau Prison for his role in the war. He published two memoirs in which he detailed the efforts to support Hartenstein's humanitarian mission while protecting U-boats from attack. He died in 1980.

GLOSSARY

bayonet—Steel blade attached to the end of a rifle, used in hand-to-hand combat.

bow—Pointed front end of a vessel or boat.

bung—Plug that seals the drainage hole in a small boat.

civilian—Person who is not a member of the military.

code—System of signals and symbols to communicate secretly.

compass—Magnetic device used to determine direction.

conning tower—Raised part of a submarine that contains periscope for navigation and the ladder for access.

convoy—Group of ships traveling together for protection against attack.

course—Route that a vessel takes to its destination.

crash dive—Submarine tactic to avoid enemies by going underwater bow first as fast as possible.

cruiser—Large, armed military ship built for speed and long distance.

davits—Cranes that project over the side of a ship and hold lifeboats or cargo.

depth charges—Bombs designed to explode underwater when they reach a certain depth.

destroyer—Military ship designed to attack other vessels with offensive weapons such as large guns and torpedoes.

drifting—When a vessel moves with the waves and wind without steering.

GRT—Gross registered tonnage, the amount of space inside a ship available to carry cargo, fuel, and people.

gunwale—Upper edge of a ship's or boat's side.

helm—Location of the steering and speed control mechanisms for a ship or submarine.

Horlick's—Tablets made of milk products, which, in a lifeboat, were meant to supply energy and vitamins.

hull—Main body of a boat, excluding any masts or sails.

keel—Bottom structural support of a boat that extends from front to back and projects into water.

knots—Nautical miles per hour, used to express speed of a vessel in water.

life belt or jacket—Flotation device that is worn like a piece of clothing, which is filled with cork or kapok and covered in canvas and fitted with straps that secure it to the body.

lifeboat—Small boat equipped with oars and possibly a sail that is used to escape a sinking ship.

life raft—Flat flotation device, often rectangular with an open center, made of metal tubes wrapped in rubber material and usually with a net covering the center. Life rafts are designed for very short-term survival in the water. (A lifeboat differs from a life raft in that its entire hull is made from a firm material such as wood or metal.)

navigation—Process of planning a route of travel using direction finding with a compass.

ocean liner—Passenger ship capable of taking hundreds of people across the ocean, such as between Liverpool and New York.

pemmican—High-protein, high-calorie spread of dried meat that has been ground into powder and mixed with fat and berries, and can be stored for a long time.

pens—Reinforced structures for repairing and resupplying U-boats.

periscope—Vertical tube with lenses and mirrors that allows a person to see an otherwise blocked view.

port—Left side of a vessel.

prisoner of war—Person captured by the enemy in a war.

propeller—Device that moves a vehicle forward using three to five angled blades that spin on a single axis.

ration—In a lifeboat, a portion determined by dividing the amount of food and water available by the number of people and calculating how many days the supplies need to last.

rudder—Underwater blade at the back of a boat that steers it.

sloop—Small armed military ships chiefly used as escorts and patrols.

starboard—Right side of a vessel.

steamer—Ship powered by steam.

stern—Back of a vessel.

torpedo—Underwater missile or projectile that is used to sink ships.

troopship—Any ship that is designated to carry soldiers, sailors, and airmen during wartime.

war diary—Record of daily positions and activities of military units.

BIBLIOGRAPHY

BOOKS

Bercuson, David J., and Holger H. Herwig. "A Hard War: Hartenstein and U-156." Chap. 13 in *Long Night of the Tankers: Hitler's War Against Caribbean Oil*. Calgary, AB: University of Calgary Press, 2014. www.jstor.org/stable/j.ctv5rdzf3.18.

Blair, Clay. *Hitler's U-Boat War: The Hunted, 1942–1945*. New York: Modern Library, 1998.

Breyer, Siegfried, and Gerhard Koop. *The German Navy at War, 1935–1945*. Vol. 2, *The U-Boat*. West Chester, PA: Schiffer, 1997.

Carruthers, Bob. *The U-Boat War in the Atlantic*. Warwickshire, UK: Coda Books, 2012.

Churchill, Winston. *Memoirs of the Second World War*. New York: Bonanza Books, 1978.

Craven, Wesley Frank, and James Lea Cate, eds. *Plans and Early Operations, January 1939 to August 1942*. Vol. 1 of *The Army Air Forces in World War II*. Washington, DC: Office of Air Force History, 1983.

Craven, Wesley Frank, and James Lea Cate, eds. "The War Against the Sub Pens." Chap. 8 in *Europe: Torch to Pointblank, August 1942 to December 1943*. Vol. 2 of *The Army*

Air Forces in World War II. Washington, DC: Office of Air Force History, 1983. archive.org/details/Vol2Europe TorchToPointblank/page/n275.

Doherty, Richard. *Churchill's Greatest Fear: The Battle of the Atlantic, 3 September 1939 to 7 May 1945*. Barnsley, UK: Pen & Sword Books, 2015.

Dönitz, Karl. *Memoirs: Ten Years and Twenty Days*. Translated by R. H. Stevens in collaboration with David Woodward. New York: Da Capo Press, 1997.

High Command of German Navy. *The U-Boat Commander's Handbook*. Translated by US Navy, 1943. Gettysburg, PA: Thomas, 1989.

Howe, George F. *Signal Intelligence in Northwest Africa and Western Europe*. Vol. 1 of *United States Cryptologic History Series IV: World War II*. Fort Meade, MD: National Security Agency, 2010. www.nsa.gov/portals/75/documents/about/cryptologic-heritage/historical-figures-publications/publications/wwii/asi_in_northwest_africa.pdf.

Jones, David C. *The Enemy We Killed, My Friend*. Llandysul, Wales: Gomer Press, 1999.

Large, Tony. *In Deep and Troubled Waters*. Donington, UK: Paul Watkins, 2001.

McLoughlin, Jim. *One Common Enemy: The* Laconia *Incident: A Survivor's Memoir*. With David Gibb. Adelaide, Australia: Wakefield Press, 2006.

Naisawald, L. VanLoan. *In Some Foreign Field: Four British Graves and Submarine Warfare on the North Carolina Outer Banks*. Raleigh: North Carolina Office of Archives and History, 1997.

Parr, Claude. *A Seemingly Ordinary Man*. With additional material by Gavin Parr. Cardiff, Wales: Candy Jar Books, 2015.

Peillard, Léonce. *The* Laconia *Affair*. Translated by Oliver Coburn. New York: G. P. Putnam's Sons, 1963.

Roskill, S. W. *The War at Sea, 1939–1945*. Vol. 1, *The Defensive*. London: Her Majesty's Stationery Office, 1954.

Roskill, S. W. *The War at Sea, 1939–1945*. Vol. 2, *The Period of Balance*. London: Her Majesty's Stationery Office, 1956.

Syrett, David, ed. *The Battle of the Atlantic and Signals Intelligence: U-Boat Situations and Trends, 1941–1945*. Publications of the Navy Records Society Vol. 139. Aldershot, UK: Ashgate, 1998. www.navyrecords.org.uk/the-battle-of-the-atlantic-and-signals-intelligence-u-boat-situations-and-trends-1941-1945/.

Werner, Herbert A. *Iron Coffins: A Personal Account of the German U-Boat Battles of World War II*. New York: Holt, Rinehart and Winston, 1969.

ARCHIVAL RECORDS

Admiralty records. National Archives. Kew, London.

Imperial War Museum Sound Archive. Oral histories of Edward Bawden, 1980; Geoffrey William Greet, December 15, 2010; Molly [Davidson] Burton, 1998; Tadeusz Walczak, March 16, 1997; and Josephine [Frame] Pratchett, n.d. www.iwm.org.uk/collections.

Jervis, W. H. Account of sinking of *Laconia*, Cunard Line, 1942. Papers of John Ronald Nice. Cunard Records. National Maritime Museum, Liverpool, England.

National Archives and Records Administration: Photo CPT James D. Harden receiving Distinguished Service Medal. catalog.archives.gov/id/204945677.

Private papers of Gen. Robert C. Richardson III provided by Robert C. Richardson IV.

Records of 343rd Bombardment Squadron. Declassified US Navy reports on *Laconia* sinking. National Archives and Records Administration, College Park, Maryland.

Turner, Nigel, dir. "The Laconia Incident." *History Undercover* episode aired September 6, 1998, History Channel. VHS, 50 mins.

ARTICLES AND OTHER ONLINE SOURCES

Avalon Project. "Nuremberg Trial Proceedings Volume 13: One Hundred Twenty-Fifth Day." Transcript of Karl Dönitz testimony, May 9, 1946. Yale Law School. avalon.law.yale.edu/imt/05-09-46.asp.

Beesly, Patrick. "Ultra and the Battle of the Atlantic: The British View." Paper presented at the Naval History Symposium, US Naval Academy, Annapolis, MD, October 28, 1977. www.nsa.gov/Portals/70/documents/news-features/declassified-documents/cryptologic-spectrum/Ultra.pdf.

Boler, David. "Churchill Proceedings—Canada and the Battle of the Atlantic." *Finest Hour* 159 (Summer 2013). International Churchill Society. winstonchurchill.org/publications/finest-hour/finest-hour-159/churchill-proceedings-canada-and-the-battle-of-the-atlantic/.

Brown, Robert J. "Operation Catapult: Naval Destruction at Mers-El-Kabir." *World War II*, September 1997. Reprinted by Historynet, August 31, 2006. www.historynet.com/operation-catapult-naval-destruction-at-mers-el-kebir.htm.

Chen, C. Peter. "Gloire." World War II Database. ww2db.com/ship_spec.php?ship_id=845.

D'Adamo, Cristiano. "Action off Calabria." Regia Marina Italiana. www.regiamarina.net/detail_text_with_list.asp.

Daily Progress (Charlottesville, VA). "Naval Battle off the Coast of Virginia." June 17, 2017. www.dailyprogress.com/article_e8aa27d4-5505-11e7-a0ae-935dbf29c50a.html.

Derencin, Robert. "Radio Communications of German U-boats in WWI and WWII." Uboat.net, April 7, 2002. uboat.net/articles/35.html.

Helgason, Gudmundur. "The War in Maps: North American Coast." Uboat.net. uboat.net/maps/us_east_coast.htm.

Hollandbeck, Andy, Jeff Nilsson, and Demaree Bess. "Not So Neutral, America's War Efforts Before Pearl Harbor." *Saturday Evening Post*, August 11, 2016. www.saturdayeveningpost.com/2016/08/not-neutral-americas-war-efforts-pearl-harbor/.

Jackson, Ashley. "Of Sea Lanes, Strategy and Logistics, Africa's Ports and Islands During the Second World War." Defence-in-Depth, King's College, London. defenceindepth.co/2014/10/09/of-sea-lanes-strategy-and-logistics-africas-ports-and-islands-during-the-second-world-war/.

JoChallacombe2. "Devon Family Saved by a U-Boat (Part 1)." WW2 People's War archive, BBC, June 24, 2005. www.bbc.co.uk/history/ww2peopleswar/stories/94/a4262294.shtml.

Kikoy, Herbert. "Destruction of the French Fleet by the British WWII—Operation Catapult." War History Online, August 29, 2018. www.warhistoryonline.com/instant-articles/operation-catapult.html.

Maurer, Maurer, ed. *Combat Squadrons of the Air Force: World War II.* US Air Force Historical Division, 1969. www.afhra.af.mil/Portals/16/documents/Studies/51-100/AFD-090601-110.pdf.

Murray, Williamson. "Why Germany's Kriegsmarine Lost the Battle of the Atlantic." April 28, 2015. Historynet. www.historynet.com/why-germanys-kriegsmarine-lost-the-battle-of-the-atlantic.htm.

National Army Museum (London). "The Struggle for North Africa." www.nam.ac.uk/explore/struggle-north-africa-1940-43.

National Museum of the US Navy. "Sinking of U-156." www.history.navy.mil/content/history/museums/nmusn/explore/photography/wwii/wwii-atlantic/battle-of-the-atlantic/engagements-german-uboats/1943-attacks-german/1943-march-8-U-156.html.

National Security Agency. *German Naval Communication Intelligence*, SRH-024. Vol. 3 of *Battle of the Atlantic.* www.history.navy.mil/research/library/online-reading-room/title-list-alphabetically/b/battle-atlantic-volume-3-german-naval-communication-iIntelligence.html#chap5.

Navy Department. *History of Convoy and Routing.* Vol 11 of *United States Naval Administration in World War II.* Washington, DC: Navy Department, [1945]. www.history.navy.mil/research/library/online-reading-room/title-list-alphabetically/h/history-convoy-routing-1945.html.

Offley, Ed. "Undefended Shore: America Anti-Submarine Operations in 1942." *Navy Times*, May 20, 2019. www.navytimes.com/news/your-navy/2019/05/20/undefended-shore-american-antisubmarine-operations-in-1942/.

Pagliero, George, dir. *The Sinking of the Laconia: Survivors' Stories.* Documentary aired January 8, 2011, on BBC Two, UK. Video clip, 5:10 mins. vimeo.com/12810123.

PBS Thirteen. Preview of "Churchill's Deadly Decision," episode 8, season 10 of *Secrets of the Dead.* April 16, 2010. www.pbs.org/wnet/secrets/churchills-deadly-decision-preview-this-episode/548/.

Pegram, F. H. War Diary of West Africa Command, March-December 1942. Transcribed by Don Kindell. Admiralty War Diaries of World War 2, Naval-History.net. www.naval-history.net/xDKWD-WAfrica1942.htm.

Raynor, Don. "My Early Years at War." WW2 People's War archive, BBC, December 27, 2005. www.bbc.co.uk/history/ww2peopleswar/stories/79/a8071779.shtml.

Roosevelt, Franklin Delano. Memorandum to Admiral Ernest King, US Navy, July 7, 1942. Franklin D. Roosevelt Presidential Library and Museum. www.fdrlibraryvirtualtour.org/graphics/07-25/7-25-FDR-to-Admiral-King.pdf.

Royal Institution of Naval Architects. "Passenger Ship Lifeboats." www.rina.org.uk/lifeboats.html.

Russell, Jerry C. "Ultra and the Campaign Against the U-Boats in World War II." Individual Study Project, US Army War College, Carlisle Barracks, PA. May 20, 1980. archive.org/details/DTIC_ADA089275/page/n3/.

"The German Naval Grid System." Uboataces.com, December 6, 2005. www.uboataces.com/articles-naval-grid.shtml.

"The Trial of Admiral Doenitz." *ONI Review* 1, no. 12 (October 1946): 26–35. www.history.navy.mil/research/library/online-reading-room/title-list-alphabetically/t/the-trial-of-admiral-doenitz.html.

U-boat Archive. "U-boat Kriegstagebücher." War diaries of U-boats 156, 506, and 507. uboatarchive.net/KTBList.htm.

ACKNOWLEDGMENTS

MICHAEL J. TOUGIAS

A big thank-you to Alison O'Leary for her research and writing. We came upon this story during the fact-finding phases for our books *So Close to Home* and *Attacked at Sea*, and it all started with a tip from Jim Hoodlet. And once again Captain Jerry Mason gave us tremendous advice while patiently steering us to eyewitness accounts of the many twists and turns of the *Laconia* story.

Deep appreciation goes to editor and publisher Christy Ottaviano. Her steady guidance, insights, and enthusiasm have helped me in so many ways.

ALISON O'LEARY

Author Alison O'Leary would like to express deep appreciation for assistance provided by the following:

- Captain Jerry Mason, US Navy (ret.), of Uboatarchive.net
- Archivist Nathaniel Patch, US National Archives, College Park, Maryland
- Staff of the National Archives, London
- Elizabeth Smith, Imperial War Museum, London

- Research room and photo archives staff of the National Maritime Museum, Liverpool, England
- Annemarie Bredow and Kai Steenbuck of Deutsches U-Boot Museum, Altenbruch, Germany
- Lisa Bradley, Oklahoma City Library
- Research assistant Paige Murray
- Mrs. Josephine Frame Pratchett
- Tim Large, son of Tony Large
- Robert C. Richardson IV, son of General Robert C. Richardson III
- Martin Lewes, son of Molly Davidson

READING GROUP GUIDE

1. How would this story be different if it happened fifty years earlier or fifty years later?
2. How would the book be different if one character were missing? Which character are you thinking about and why was their role important?
3. Tony Large survived when most people in his lifeboat perished. What factors played a role in his survival?
4. The survivors of the *Laconia* endured incredible hardships. How do you think you would react under the same conditions?
5. If you could ask one character from this book two questions, who would you choose and what would you ask?
6. Admiral Donitz was worried that his U-boats were exposed to enemy aircraft during the rescue,

yet he allowed them to proceed. Did he make a mistake? Should he not have risked the lives of his own men during war?

7. Doris Hawkins is a remarkable character. How would you describe her? Was she a hero?
8. If you had to choose an alternative title for the book, what would it be?
9. What did you know about this time period before you read the book?
10. Does this story change the way you think about war, or enemies, or humanity?
11. What other books have you read about this time period and how do they compare to this one?
12. How is this story relevant today?
13. Did your opinion of the story change as you were reading it?
14. What was the biggest surprise when reading *Abandon Ship!* and why?
15. What will you remember most about this story?

DON'T MISS!

Turn the page for a sneak preview!

PITCHPOLED

The crew of the *Fair Wind* looked out at seas that only a handful of people on earth have ever seen. It was now 11:00 a.m., and the waves had climbed to an unimaginable sixty to seventy feet of cresting fury.

The boat's location, right on the edge of the continental shelf on Georges Bank, was the very worst place to be. As the waves came off the deep water of the Atlantic and hit shallower waters on the shelf, they grew steeper, and the steeper the wave, the more likely it is to break upon itself and whatever else lies in its path. The waves were so enormous that they literally could not support themselves. The tops broke free of the main body of the wave and plunged straight downward, like an avalanche falling off a cliff. The wind, spiking at seventy-eight knots per hour, added its blows to the giant waves by tearing off what was left of the wave top and flinging it through the air horizontally.

Despite the terrific beating, the men of the *Fair Wind* had faith in their boat. There was no sense of panic, just a sense of awe at the power of the storm and an impatience for it to move on. The sturdy little boat continued to meet every monstrous wave, and with a little help from Ernie on the throttle, it climbed up, up, up, ever higher until its bow was out of the water at the top of the wave. There was a split-second pause as the vessel hung on the crest of each wave with its propellers out of the water, spinning wildly and uselessly in the air and foam. Then, with the bow pointed downward, Ernie backed off the throttle and down the boat went, hitting the trough in a spray of water that shot upward like a geyser. Then, clenching the wheel, Ernie saw the next wave coming and gave the engine more diesel, as he positioned the bow yet again to take the wave head-on.

Ernie may not have noticed it, but over the last couple of hours the interval between each wave had gotten shorter, allowing less and less time to recover from each punch. The crew felt like boxers in a ring, the ocean a quick, relentless opponent. They assumed they were suffering the storm's strongest punches, but in reality these waves were only jabs. The storm was still holding back.

Much of the time all Ernie could see out the windshield was foam and spray, but he had a sense of the spacing and timing between the waves, and he did his best to get ready for the next one. The vessel was doing almost everything Ernie asked of it, and with Billy's instructions, the crew felt they could weather this monster.

No serious thought was given to donning survival suits because the men, while concerned and exhausted, didn't feel any impending doom. Nor did they want to be encumbered by the suits, which made movement slow. The suit's mitten-like hand coverings would make it difficult to pilot the boat or perform other tasks that had to be done in a split second.

Billy called the *Sea Fever* again, and this time the radio static made it difficult to hear Peter Brown. But at least he knew the vessel was still afloat when Peter's garbled voice responded. Billy also heard from another fishing boat, the *Broadbill*. He wouldn't wish this storm on even his worst enemy, but it was comforting to know he wasn't facing it alone. While it would be extremely difficult to maneuver to a boat in distress, Billy knew that all three boats would give it a try in an emergency.

Billy had been through the stress of combat in Vietnam, and what was now happening on Georges Bank had a similar feel. His senses were in overdrive, and he felt wary, particularly because his enemy—the unrelenting waves—was impossible to predict. Sometimes they hit the boat from a slightly different angle; sometimes they came packed tightly together; and sometimes the waves varied in size.

For six hours, Billy had been watching the huge dark walls of water advance toward the *Fair Wind*, and just when he thought they were due for a lull, more enormous waves rose out of the gloom. He wasn't saying much to the crew simply because there was nothing to say and nothing more they could do. They just had to stay sharp, be ready to react, and ride it out.

Ernie had been manning the wheel since 8:00 a.m., so Billy decided to take the next shift around 11:30. The wind, unbelievably, was not abating, but still increasing in speed, now hitting an incredible eighty-seven knots miles per hour. Billy took the wheel while in a trough, and Ernie stood beside him to port. On the opposite side of Billy, Rob Thayer stood ready to do whatever the skipper asked of him. Dave Berry was still in his bunk below.

Peering out the windshield, Ernie's face went pale, and his eyes widened as the tallest wave yet, a wall of water as big as a ten-story building, close to one hundred feet tall, roared toward the *Fair Wind*. Billy held steady on the wheel and pushed the throttle for more power, and the boat started to climb the vertical slope. None of the three men said a word, but all three must have been thinking the same thing, hoping to coax the *Fair Wind* forward. *Come on, come on. Climb!*

As the vessel reached the halfway point up the wave, it seemed the propellers stopped biting because of all the foam, and Billy strained forward, willing his boat to climb still higher.

For a half second, the boat hung on the face of the wave. Then the men, wide-eyed with terror, watched the curling summit of the wave top collapse on them. There was no time to shout, only a split second to brace themselves, as tons of churning water crashed directly onto the *Fair Wind.*

The impact, sounding like an explosion, spun the vessel 180 degrees like a toy. Anything not bolted down went flying, and the three men in the pilothouse struggled to remain standing and avoid getting slammed into the walls or windshields. Dave Berry, still below, was likely hurled out of his bunk and into the air before crashing into the bunks opposite his.

In those agonizing slow-motion seconds, Ernie felt a sickening sensation as the *Fair Wind* careened wildly down the very wave it had tried to climb. The boat was in free fall, accelerating from the force of the wave on its stern. Its nose smacked into the trough below, striking the ocean with incredible force. The bow bored into the sea, and Ernie felt the stern of the vessel, propelled by the avalanching wave behind the boat, go whipping up and over the submerged bow. Ernie smashed into the pilothouse ceiling, which was now below him. The *Fair Wind* had "pitchpoled," flipped end over end, and was now upside down.

Thousands of gallons of frigid water poured into the wheelhouse, seizing the men in a swirling embrace. In only a second or two, the upside-down wheelhouse had almost completely filled with green seawater. Stunned, Ernie was tossed about as if in a washing machine. It was wet, cold, and dark, but he instinctively pushed upward and hit his head on the wheelhouse floor, where four or five inches of air had become trapped. Although he was totally disoriented, uncertain if he was upside down or right side up, his brain still screamed, *Get out, get out!*

Ernie took what air he could and ducked his head into the water to try to figure out where he was. Below, he saw a faint patch of light. Deciding to swim for it, Ernie dove but hit his head on what may have been the windshield. He turned to go back for more air. But the air pocket had vanished.

Ernie thought to himself, It's all over. So this is how it happens. I'll be dead in a couple of minutes. Amazingly, he did not panic, nor shrink from confronting his death. He simply thought, *If it's going to happen, it happens.*

The survival instinct, however, is strong, and Ernie was not about to help the ocean do its dirty work. He still had one option left—besides giving up—and that was to go back down and swim toward the light.

Operating on adrenaline, he dove yet again, hoping the faint patch of light was an opening and not just a windshield. With lungs screaming for air, he slipped through a small hole. As soon as he felt his legs free of the boat, he looked in the direction he thought was the surface and stroked and kicked with all his strength. He couldn't hold his breath much longer. Ernie clawed his way through the water, knowing that if he didn't surface in a second or two, he would lose consciousness.

The upward climb seemed an eternity, but just before Ernie felt he would either breathe in the ocean or black out, his head cleared the surface. As he gasped for air, a wave washed over him. He kicked furiously to raise his head a bit higher. Even when his head was above the wave, breathing was difficult because of the foam in the air. He was taking both air and water into his lungs.

Ernie saw the hull of the *Fair Wind*, and for a second this sight seemed so surreal, so strange, that his mind could not grasp what had happened. Amazingly, the boat's propeller still whirled at full speed, but Ernie couldn't hear the whine of the propeller over the howling wind and crashing seas. He had emerged on the windward side of the vessel, and he tried to grip the overturned hull. It was impossible, however, to secure a handhold on the smooth, slick metal.

Although Ernie tried to stay with the vessel, the wind drove the boat away faster than he could swim. He experienced a sense of deep dread; his only hope for survival was drifting along with the boat.

All manner of debris, from lines to smashed pieces of wood, was swirling around as Ernie fought to stay with the boat, but with each passing second the *Fair Wind* was pushed farther away. Just staying afloat became a struggle for Ernie with his boots and jacket weighing him down. Fortunately, his boots were untied and he kicked them free, and then he squirmed out of his jacket.

Exhausted, and barely able to move his arms, Ernie spotted a bucket floating nearby and grabbed it; he turned it over to trap some air inside and used it as a float. The full magnitude of what had happened now hit him like a blow to the stomach. The situation looked hopeless, and already the cold November seas of 55 degrees were sucking the warmth out of his body and sapping what little strength he had left.

In a strange way, however, in those first few moments after capsizing, Ernie had already been lucky several times. First, he had stayed conscious, despite being thrown about in the pilothouse. Second, the fact that he did not have a survival suit on saved his life: its buoyancy would have prevented him from swimming downward toward the opening in the pilothouse. And, when he did surface, it was away from the slicing propeller. He also had the good fortune to have his boots untied or he would have surely sunk under their weight. And finally, the bucket had floated within reach as if guided there by the very wind and waves that had pitchpoled the *Fair Wind.*

Yes, a few small strokes of luck fell Ernie's way, but now, with the boat drifting away and Ernie fighting to stay afloat in the unrelenting seas, he was going to need more than luck to survive; he'd need a miracle.

Lindsey Potter

MICHAEL J. TOUGIAS is the author of many award-winning true rescue stories, including the *New York Times* bestseller *The Finest Hours*, *A Storm Too Soon*, *Into the Blizzard*, and *Attacked at Sea*, as well as the young reader's adaptation of *In Harm's Way* by Doug Stanton. A frequent lecturer, Tougias splits his time between Massachusetts and Florida. He invites you to visit him online at michaeltougias.com.

Tony Mistretta

ALISON O'LEARY is an award-winning journalist based in New England. She is a former correspondent for the *Boston Globe* and the coauthor with Michael J. Tougias of *Attacked at Sea*. She invites you to visit her online at alisonoleary.com.

STORIES OF TRUE SURVIVAL

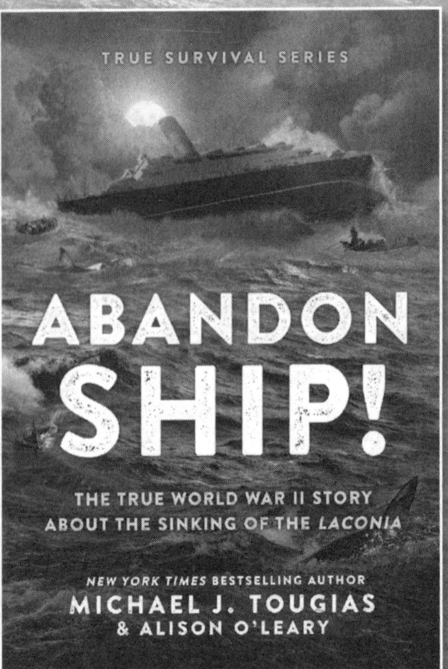

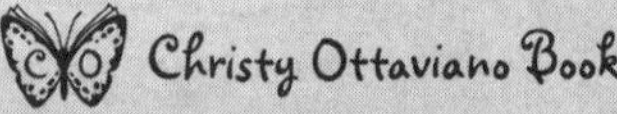

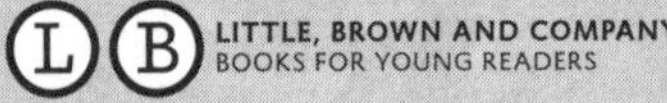

LBYR.com

BOB 11